Indians in Guyana

A concise history from their arrival to the present

En Letitia

Basdeo Mangru

Adams Press, Chicago, Illinois

ACKNOWLEDGMENTS. The Author would like to thank the following for permission to reproduce photographs and maps, and to use materials from their publications:

Guyana Journal, History Today, Indian Frontiers, Release, Collins Press, Hansib Publishing Ltd., TSAR Publications. Warwick University Caribbean Studies, the Rajkumari Cultural Center, the University of Guyana Library.

The published/unpublished works of the following have provided useful information for this study: Frank Birbalsingh, Sr. Mary Noel-Menezes, Brian Moore, Robert Moore, Tyran Ramnarine, Clem Seecharan, Gora Singh.

ISBN 0-9670093-0-8
Library of Congress Catalog Number 99-068806

Printed in the United States of America

Published by Adams Press

For information contact the Author
109-41 115th Street
Richmond Hill, NY 11420

Foreword

In his latest work on the nature, scope and extent of the role played by the people of India in the life of Guyana, Dr. Basdeo Mangru ties together themes from his previous books and more than twenty articles, and provides us with a panoramic view of the reasons for the migration of Indians to Guyana, the system of recruitment for the exodus from India, the conditions of the voyage, the working and living conditions of the Indians in Guyana, their religious practices and other aspects of their social life, and their contributions to the development of Guyana. The work concludes with an analysis of their "second migration" to the United States of America and problems of adjustment.

Apart from the value of this study as a contribution to multicultural history, it provides a guide for the descendants of these early travelers to trace their roots, to appreciate the history and culture of Indians from the Caribbean, and to have available a supplement to high school and college texts which omit detailed treatment of this sorely neglected but culturally rich community.

Hopefully, it will form the basis for new courses on both the high school and college level, which, of course, Dr. Mangru is most qualified to teach.

Jules S. Zimmerman, Ph.D.
Social Studies Chairman
John Adams High School

To the *jahajis* and their descendants

They (Indians) were pioneers. They suffered in the mud. They worked day and night. Rain came and wet them; the sun came and dried them. They would get up at four o'clock in the morning, and walk miles to the backdam without any transportation to take them. They carried their saucepan with a little rice and pieces of bora or a piece of squash, and they sat down about half past eleven to eat by the trench corner, after which they would wash their saucepan and use it to drink trench water. It was **they** who built Guyana prior to 1964.

Robert Janki
In *From Pillar to Post*

Contents

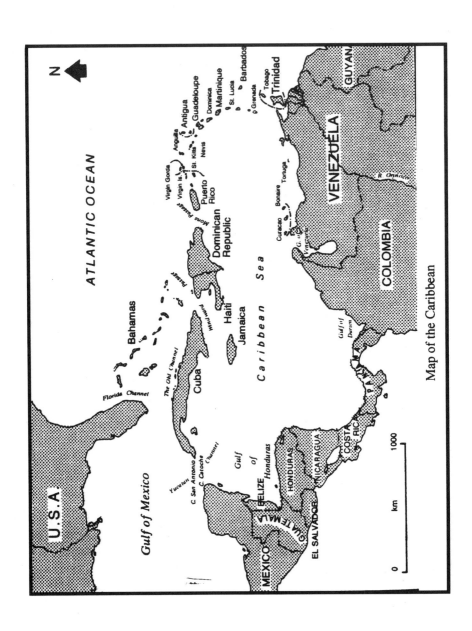

Map of the Caribbean

Introduction

This concise history of the experiences of (East) Indians in Guyana (formerly British Guiana) is geared for the general reader, high school students and those with an interest in their roots. Previous studies on the Indians in the Caribbean mainly targeted academics and students researching the field.

The study is undertaken for four main reasons. First, it is in response to the lack of readily available literature on these enterprising people. Second, it will supplement the Social Studies curriculum on South Asia and Latin America in the New York City (NYC) high schools. Third, it will expand the options in the limited number of Social Studies electives now available to high school students. For this reason a list of power aims for teachers is provided. Currently, the history and culture of South Asians in the Caribbean is hardly taught despite an increasing enrollment of students from that group in the NYC high school system and a growing interest in the field. Fourthly, it will enable the Caribbean Examination Council (CXC) to add another theme to its syllabus, giving Caribbean students a wider choice in areas of concentration.

This book begins with an historical background of Guyana and an examination of the situation in the Caribbean following the abolition of slavery. It then goes on to discuss social and economic conditions in India which led Indians to leave their villages for employment overseas. It describes the recruiting system and conditions on the voyage. It then focuses on the experiences of Indians in Guyana from their arrival in 1838 to the present. The reasons for their 'second migration' and their adjustment to life in NYC are also briefly examined. The book provides a bird's eye view of practically all aspects of the lives of these resilient people. It is written in clear, simple language and is both readable and informative.

Guyana has a population of about 800,000 and an area of 83,000 square miles. The population comprises East Indians (over 50%), Africans (about 40%), Amerindians, Chinese, Portuguese

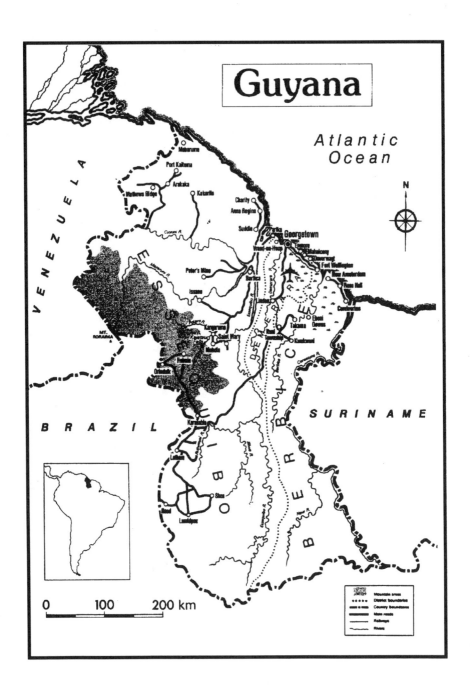

Guyana

Atlantic Ocean

VENEZUELA

BRAZIL

SURINAME

MT. RORAIMA

Mabaruma
Port Kaituma
Arakaka
Mathews Ridge
Kokerita
Charity
Anna Regina
Suddie
Parika
Georgetown
Vreed-en-Hoop
Mahaicony
Fort Wellington
New Amsterdam
Rose Hall
Peter's Mine
Bartica
Issano
Enmore
Kwakwani
Canefield
Ekeni Downs
Takama
Kangaruma
Saint Mary
Mahdia
Orinduik
Karasabai
Lethem
Shea
Annai
Lumidpasi

ESSEQUIBO DEMERARA BERBICE

0   100   200 km

	Mountain areas
	District boundaries
	Country boundaries
	Main roads
	Railways
	Rivers

8

and Europeans. The official language is English but Creolese or pidgin English is widely spoken. The three main religions are Hinduism, Christianity and Islam. Guyana is a democracy headed by a President elected for a term of five years. It has a unicameral (one-house) legislature, the National Assembly, which is elected under a system of Proportional Representation. The backbone of Guyana's economy is agriculture with sugar and rice being the main products. Bauxite and gold mining, forestry and fishery also form an important part of the economy.

It is estimated that in the indenture period (1838-1917) roughly one million workers from India migrated to over a dozen countries in different parts of the world. They went mainly to Mauritius (453,063), Guyana (238,979), Trinidad (143,939), Fiji (60,000), Jamaica (36,412) and Suriname (34,304). Smaller batches also went to Natal in South Africa and other British and French Caribbean Islands. By the time the indenture system officially ended in 1920, thousands had returned to India. The majority, however, remained in the sugar colonies and built permanent homes. Today, Indians form majorities in Mauritius, Fiji, Guyana and Trinidad, and large communities in Suriname, East Africa and South East Asia.

Historical background

Guyana, the land of many rivers, was first settled by the Amerindians, a people of Asian stock. The coming of Europeans stemmed from the third voyage of Columbus who sailed along the Guyanese coast in 1498. But it was the tale of El Dorado, the gilded one, a hundred years later, which attracted European settlement. The vision of immense wealth dominated the life of Sir Walter Raleigh for over 25 years only to end in his execution in England.

The Dutch also showed an interest in the region and about 1616 they established a settlement at Fort Kyk-over-al on the Essequibo River. It was during the period of Dutch occupation that British sugar planters, mostly from Barbados, came to Guyana and cultivation shifted from cotton and coffee to sugar. Because the coastlands were below sea level, the Dutch developed an elaborate system of polders for water control. On 23 February, 1763 one of the most violent slave revolts began. Known as the Berbice Slave Rebellion, it was an attempt by the slave leader, Cuffy, and his 'generals' to get rid of the slave system. After a year of resistance, the rebellion was crushed and the leaders hanged.

Towards the end of the 18th century, particularly during the American Revolution (1776-1783) and the French Revolution (1789), Guyana was controlled at different times by the British, French and Dutch. In 1814 the three colonies (now counties) of Essequibo, Demerara and Berbice were finally handed over to Britain. They remained separate until 1831 when they were united to form the colony of British Guiana with Georgetown (formerly Stabroek) as its capital. The British remained in control until 1966 when independence was granted and the colony renamed Guyana.

The constitution, which the British inherited from the Dutch, provided for a Court of Policy (law making body) and a Combined Court (financial body). Under slavery, membership to these bodies was restricted to those who owned at least 80 acres of land of which 40 must be under cultivation. To be eligible to vote, a person must own at least 25 slaves. Afterwards he must have an income of at least 2,001 guilders (one guilder = 32 cents). As a result, the ordinary man was excluded from voting and from holding office. The planters thus had both economic and political control and they used it to ensure that the sugar interests remained powerful. Although there were some changes in the constitution in 1891 and 1928, the planters continued to maintain power until independence.

Effects of emancipation

The emancipation (freedom) of slaves in 1834 affected the sugar colonies in the Caribbean in two ways. In the smaller islands like Barbados and Antigua, where little land space was available for agriculture, the ex-slaves (Creoles or Blacks) had to continue working on the plantations (estates) or starve. It was in the larger territories of Guyana, Jamaica and Trinidad that problems arose. The sugar planters in Guyana feared that the ex-slaves would leave the plantations and squat on the banks of rivers and creeks. This would result in a shortage of labor, higher wage demands and the collapse of the plantations. In fact, several gangs of ex-slaves were reportedly moving from estate to estate demanding their 'price' for a given job.

The planters, therefore, took certain steps to keep workers on their plantations. They passed laws to prevent squatting and set the price of land so high that hardly any laborer could purchase a plot. However, land became available when many sugar, coffee and cotton plantations were abandoned in the 1840s. Many laborers, especially headmen, pooled their resources to buy these plantations. Thus began the 'Village Movement' and a slow flow of workers from the plantations to the villages.

The first communal village in Guyana was established in 1839 when 83 laborers bought Plantation Northbrook on the East Coast Demerara, which they renamed Victoria in honor of the Queen. By 1848 a number of villages had been formed from the Corentyne to the Pomeroon and over one-half (44,000) of the work force of 84,915 had settled on them. There was thus a shortage of labor for certain types of field work, particularly weeding and manuring.

Immigration schemes

The sugar planters attempted to solve their labor problems through various means. Those with some capital introduced new technology (vacuum pans, megass carriers, juice extractors) to reduce their dependence on wage labor. Others tried to cut expenses by reducing wages which resulted in a 'General Strike' in 1842 and another in 1848. The majority, however, believed that immigration would solve all their problems. Through immigration they would have control over labor and this would enable them to reduce wages as well. By introducing workers from different parts of the world, the planters hoped to divide the work force and

11

prevent any combination against them. Accordingly, they passed several resolutions with a view to increasing the labor supply.

Between 1834 and 1890 the planters introduced immigrants from different parts of the world -- the West Indian islands (41,017), the Portuguese islands of Madeira and the Azores (32,216), Malta (208), southern United States (70), West Africa (14,060), China (13,533), Europe (381) and India.

The expectations of the sugar planters with regard to many of these workers were not met. The Portuguese and the Maltese suffered from neglect, exposure to the sun and tropical diseases. Opposition to emigration from the West Indian Islands and from West Africa prevented large numbers from leaving their homelands. Those from southern United States were suspicious of emigration as they believed that plantation agriculture was similar to slavery. The problem with Chinese immigration was the high cost of importation and the scarcity of Chinese women immigrants. The planters were also disappointed with those who settled as many turned to gambling and opium smoking.

It was India with its millions in heavily populated areas which became the main source of labor. Between 1851 and 1917 the flow to Guyana from India was uninterrupted. When Indian immigration came to an end, 238,979 Indians had been introduced. During this period 65,538 claimed a free return passage at the end of their contract. Hundreds, however, remigrated after spending a short time in India.

Immigration into Guyana was financed through the colony's Immigration Fund. The planters contributed two-thirds to the expenses of the fund which included passage costs, payment to surgeons and the cost of sending Indians home at the end of the contract. The colony contributed one-third which included the salary of the Immigration Agent at Calcutta and the expenses of running the Immigration Department. The colony also paid the cost of maintaining Indians in hospitals and other public institutions.

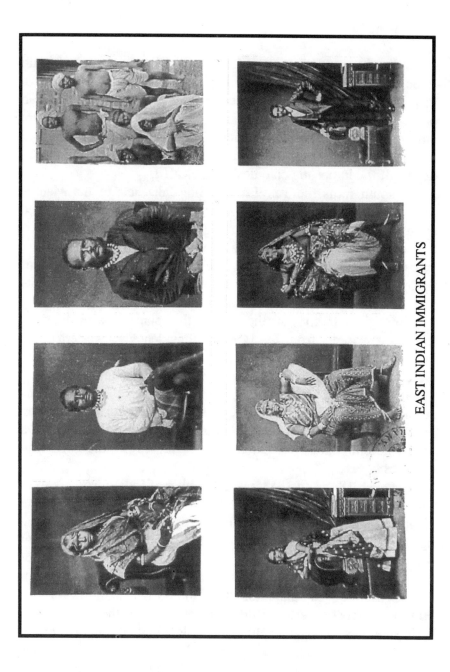

EAST INDIAN IMMIGRANTS

Origins of Indians

Indian workers came from different districts in north and south India. In north India the main districts were the North-Western Provinces and Oudh or the United Provinces (today Uttar Pradesh or U.P.). Bengal, Bihar and, to a limited extent, the Punjab were other important recruiting districts. These workers were shipped overseas from the port of Calcutta around which the emigration depots of the importing colonies were located.

In south India the Tamil and Telinga districts of the Madras Presidency were the main suppliers. The workers were shipped from the port of Madras. The immigration of Madrasis, however, ended in the 1860s, although small batches did arrive in the closing years of indenture. In 1870 Madrasis comprised a mere 14% of those imported from India. Thus the majority of Indian immigrants were from the north of the sub-continent.

Towards the end of the 1850s the planters also tried to introduce workers from the Bombay Presidency in western India but without success. The Bombay Government argued that there were no unemployment problems in the Presidency and that it would be difficult to induce Indians to emigrate overseas. This strong opposition convinced Guyanese planters not to set up an agency to recruit workers from the Bombay Presidency. As a result, no emigrants were shipped from Bombay to the Caribbean colonies.

Between 1838 and 1858 a large number of Indian workers were 'hill coolies' (Dhangars, Mundas, Kols, Oraons) from Chota Nagpur, a sub-division of the Bengal Presidency. This source dried up because of their high mortality at sea and heavy demands for their labor by the tea planters of Assam, a far closer destination for them. The 'hill coolies' were used chiefly to clear the jungle for the extension of tea cultivation. The Bhojpuri-speaking (a form of Hindi) districts of western Bihar and eastern U.P. then became the main suppliers. Altogether Bihar and U.P. supplied roughly 86% of the recruits to Guyana. The district of Basti in U.P. contributed the largest percentage (8.7%) of recruits to the colony.

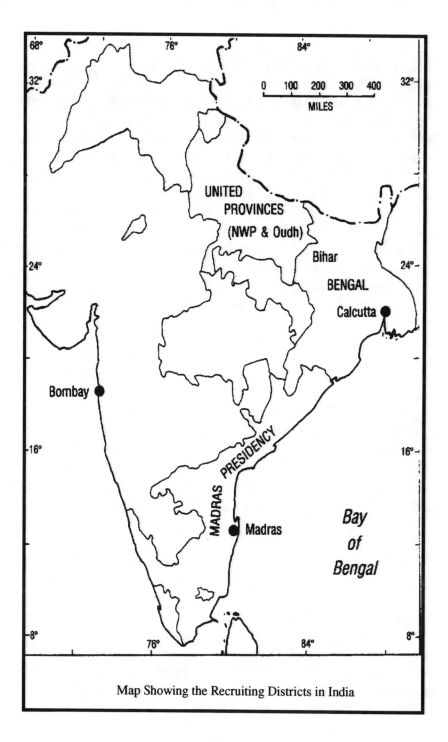

Map Showing the Recruiting Districts in India

There were three main reasons why Indians left their homelands to work overseas. The British rulers introduced changes in India which affected all aspects of life. The new system of land tenure and the importation of cheap, machine-made products from England created many problems. The Indian village handicraft industries suffered terribly. Hundreds of thousands of villagers lost their traditional livelihood and turned to agriculture for a living. But because agriculture was seasonal, thousands were either unemployed or underemployed. The problem was made worse by a steady growth of population in already overcrowded areas. During the off-season thousands would leave their homes for employment in the industrial areas of Calcutta. Journeying for many days on bullock carts, those who failed to find ready employment or had no money became easy prey to recruiters.

The frequent famines also resulted in the movement of population from one place to another. During famines villagers often became desperate and entire villages would be deserted. As such, thousands would go to the emigration depots and enlist so as to avoid starvation. It was during this time that villagers would emigrate with their families.

A third factor was the Indian Mutiny of 1857. Some of the *sepoys* (Indian soldiers in the army of the British East India Company) who rebelled against British rule, emigrated overseas rather than face imprisonment at Port Blair in the Andamans. Thus Indian emigration overseas resulted from 'push' rather than 'pull' factors. The distant Caribbean sugar colonies did not provide much attraction to Indian workers.

Recruitment

Throughout the period of Indian emigration to the sugar colonies, the recruiting system remained uniform. Emigrants were enlisted by licensed recruiters who were assisted by unlicensed men called *arkatis* in north India and *maistris* in south India. After enticing a batch of villagers, the *arkati* handed them to the licensed recruiter, received his commission and left immediately to entrap

The Emigrants at their meal.

others. The licensed recruiter took the recruits to the subagent (largely British and Indian) who manned the subdepot. These subdepots were set up in the 1860s when recruiting operations shifted from Bengal to Bihar and U.P. The subagent arranged for registration before the magistrate of the district. At registration, the emigrants were often asked in gangs whether they knew their destination and were willing to emigrate. Mixed in these gangs were recruiters who often shouted "yes." Thus many Indians were registered without knowing where they were going to or the terms of the contract.

There were several abuses in the recruiting system. Kidnapping, deceit, forced detention and enticing recruits away from one depot to another took place on a regular basis. Recruits were hardly informed about their destination or the type of work they would be required to do. They were not told that they would have to cross the sea *(kala pani)* which to Hindus meant loss of caste and grave social problems. Recruiters also enlisted workers in one district and registered them in another so that the circumstances of recruitment could not be detected. Indian women were often the main victims as they were afraid to protest against malpractice. Although recruiters could be dismissed or imprisoned for abuses or irregularities, recruiting malpractices continued throughout the period.

Following registration the emigrants, accompanied by *chaprasis*, were taken by train from north India to the main depot at Calcutta. During this long journey (for example, 685 miles from Kanpur to Calcutta) recruits were influenced by others and many often deserted at different train stations. On arrival, they were medically examined and those suffering from contagious diseases were either rejected or sent to a hospital for treatment. All rejects were sent back to the place of recruitment at the agency's expense. During their stay at the depot, which varied from a few days to as long as six months because of recruiting difficulties, recruits were regularly examined and 'seasoned' for the long voyage overseas.

At embarkation the emigrants were issued a supply of warm clothing, and a copy of the registration certificate was given to the

Medical examination of New arrivals

captain of the ship. This registration certificate, containing such information as name, age, place of birth, caste, next of kin, bodily marks and name of ship, was given to the authorities on arrival in the importing colony. These certificates are filed in the national archives of each recipient colony where a copy can be obtained once information such as name of ship and year of arrival is known.

The voyage

Throughout the 19th century sailing ships, which covered the voyage in about three or four months, were used to convey immigrants. In addition to passengers, who were allowed to carry *dholaks* (small drums), the ships were loaded with rice, dal, chillies and other commodities consumed by Indians. Besides the officers and crew, each ship had compounders (those who dispensed medicines), interpreters and *topazees* or sweepers. Very often interpreters on ships were later employed by the sugar planters as clerks and interpreters in the Immigration Department.

Throughout the voyage certain precautions were taken to prevent contact between the crew and Indian women. Nevertheless, a few assaults on Indian women by the ship's crew did occur. A rare event took place in 1883 when Dr. T.D. Atkins, Surgeon-General of the *Silhet*, married an Indian woman, Janky. To maintain discipline, there were separate compartments for married and single immigrants. Each batch of 25 immigrants was under the control of a *sirdar* or headman who supervised food distribution and sanitary arrangements.

During the early period of immigration mortality on the voyage was high largely because of cholera and fevers. From the 1860s many innovations were introduced to reduce the number of deaths. The authorities began to hire experienced surgeons to provide better health care, and trained cooks to prepare nutritious food. They also improved the quality of drinking water by installing a water distilling apparatus. All these tended to reduce the death rate. By the first decade of the 20th century steam ships, which covered the voyage in less than two months, were regularly used. Consequently, the death rate was further reduced. Between 1871 and 1890 it averaged only 2.22 %, and this low death rate continued to the end of the system.

The plantation system

Indian workers landed in Guyana and other sugar colonies with many handicaps. Although they had usable skills, the majority were poor and illiterate and were not physically strong to perform the work demanded of them. They had little knowledge of the English language which placed them at a disadvantage. They were discriminated against as they were the only group required to carry 'passes' to establish their identity. They could not even choose their employer or the plantation to which they were assigned. They were isolated on the plantation and denied almost every amenity of life. In contrast, the planters, who were mainly Scottish or English, exercised both political and economic control. They made the laws that governed all aspects of the lives of workers.

Shortly after arrival, Indians came under the discipline of the plantation system. The plantation was seen as a world of its own and it governed the lives of every one within it. The work force was made up of both skilled and unskilled workers whose movements were closely monitored. Plantation society was rigidly divided with the Whites occupying the highest positions and the workers the lowest. According to West Indian historian, Elsa Goveia, the plantation under slavery was "a small world, and the field slave was trapped in this world like a fly in a spider's web." Little had changed in this former slave society when Indians began arriving in large numbers.

The 'Gladstone Experiment'

On 4 January, 1836 John Gladstone, father of William Gladstone (then England's future Prime Minister) and owner of Plantations Vreed-en-Hoop and Vreed-es-stein in West Demerara, wrote a letter to the Calcutta firm of Gillander, Arbuthnot and Company. He asked whether the firm could provide 100 laborers for his plantations on contracts for between five and seven years. The firm, which was supplying Indian workers to the planters in Mauritius in the Indian Ocean, saw no difficulty in sending the number requested as Indians seemed ignorant of the journey and conditions of service. The reply set the stage for the fraud and deceit which crept into the system. Gladstone then wrote the Secretary of State for the Colonies in London for permission to import Indians on five year contracts.

Permission was granted after certain safeguards were obtained. And so on 5 May, 1838 the *Whitby* and the *Hesperus* landed in Guyana with a cargo of 396 Indians, 18 having died on the voyage. Only 22 or 5% were women. Thus began Indian indentured immigration which would continue for nearly 80 years.

The first reports on these workers, the majority of whom being 'hill coolies', were favorable. They were described as simple, docile and hardworking. Those on Gladstone's estates were reportedly "a fine, healthy body of men -- they are beginning to marry or cohabit with the Negresses -- and to take pride in their dress -- the few words of English they know proved that 'Sahib' was good to them."

However, within a year several cases of neglect and beatings were reported. Some Indians were flogged with a cat-o'-nine tails and salt pickle was rubbed on their backs. This illtreatment of Indians was reported in a booklet entitled *Hill Coolies* written by John Scoble, Secretary of the British Antislavery Society. Scoble wrote: "To detail the whole of the iniquities practised on the wretched coolies ... would fill a volume." Roughly 18 months after their arrival 67, or 17% of those introduced, had died. As a result of criticism in England and in India, Indian immigration was suspended in 1839.

Bengalis and Madrasis

During the first two decades of emigration from India, both Bengalis (from north India) and Madrasis (from south India) left their villages under similar regulations. There were, however, striking differences between these two groups as regards mortality at sea and work on the sugar estates.

In the 20 years, 1838-1858, deaths among Bengalis on the voyage from Calcutta to the Caribbean were 3 times higher than among Madrasis, and 17 times more in the 1856/57 season. Emigration officials cited several reasons for the difference. They claimed that drinking water for the voyage was of a better quality at Madras than at Calcutta. At Calcutta drinking water, which was obtained from the Hughli River, was heavily polluted leading to frequent outbreaks of cholera.

The place from where the emigrants were recruited was another factor. Bengalis generally were recruited inland and were closely attached to their villages. They also suffered from depression and sea-sickness. Moreover, caste restrictions prevented them from eating certain types of food. Madrasis, in contrast, were recruited from villages near to the sea and were accustomed to sea travel. They were also more active on the voyage and seemed to eat any type of food. Hence deaths on the voyage were lower among Madrasis.

Emigration arrangements at Calcutta and Madras were also different. At Madras special precautions were taken to ensure that emigrant ships were seaworthy, that food and water were of good quality and that experienced surgeons were employed. At the depot, emigrants were carefully examined and those stricken with diseases were quarantined. Similar precautions were also taken at Calcutta but because of the large number of emigrants exported, it was not always possible to identify those suffering from contagious diseases. Moreover, in order to keep expenses down, officials at Calcutta were anxious to embark emigrants as quickly as possible. The 'seasoning process' was, therefore, shorter. As a result, deaths on Calcutta ships were often higher than those on Madras ships.

On the plantations in Guyana a complete change occurred. The Bengalis, who seemed familiar with agricultural work, acclimatized better than the Madrasis. Bengalis were seen by sugar planters as industrious workers who proved valuable in such tasks as weeding and clearing the fields. Hence north India became the main source of labor.

Although some Madrasis performed satisfactory work, all were considered poor workers from the arrival of the first batch in 1845. The planters complained that Madrasis often broke their contracts and were prone to rum drinking. Moreover, they tended to leave the plantations at the end of their contract. This situation arose because on some estates there were no hospitals. This forced Indians to travel long distances to seek medical help in Georgetown and New Amsterdam, the two main towns in Guyana. As a result, deaths among Madrasis on estates were generally higher than among Bengalis.

Those Madrasis who remained on estates seemed to excel in such jobs as clearing irrigation trenches of weeds and picking up canes which fell off *punts*. The Madrasis were, and still are, the "fishermen of British Guiana" whose chief occupation was fishing in the sea or along the banks of rivers. The industrious Madrasis who settled at Plantation Albion in Berbice also purchased small farms and raised stock. Those who came during the closing years of indenture were also considered good workers.

In contrast to north India, emigration from Madras was short-lived. It began in 1845 and ended in 1863, although some Madrasis arrived in 1913. The difference in mortality at sea between Madrasis and Bengalis was exactly the reverse on the plantations. James Crosby, Immigration Agent-General, summed up the movement from Madras: "The immigrants bore the voyage well, but they acclimatized very badly."

The indenture system

When Indian immigration was reopened in 1845, the planters began to fight for long contracts or indentures. They argued that long contracts would enable them to supervise the immigrants better and to reduce mortality as well. They claimed that they could not make the required amount of sugar since many workers preferred to fish or cultivate their own kitchen gardens. After resisting for some time, the British Government approved long contracts. All Indian workers introduced after 1862 were indentured for 5 years but they could only claim a free return passage after 10 years under contract. They could, however, return home at the end of 5 years but at their own expense.

The indenture system placed two weapons in the hands of employers. One was the Labor Law which provided for fines and imprisonment for not completing five tasks per week, for refusing to work and for absenting from work. Any worker who absented from work for seven consecutive days was considered a deserter, an offense punishable by a fine of $24 (about 6 months' pay) or a month's imprisonment. Moreover, his contract could be extended to twice the period spent in jail.

Indeed, task work placed Indian workers at a grave disadvantage. The task, which was valued at 24 cents, was measured by what the stronger Creole workers could perform in seven or eight hours. When Indians arrived, they were put to do the same amount of work in the same period of time. Being less physically stronger than the Creole, Indians generally found task work too demanding. The majority could not complete the weekly five tasks, or earn the minimum of $1.20 a week, and were thus liable to punishment.

The other weapon was the Vagrancy Law which controlled the movements of indentured workers. Under this law Indians could be arrested by the police if found two miles away from the plantation without a 'pass' signed by the manager. Indeed, the 'pass' system was used to prevent Indians from knowing the variation of wages paid on different estates, and from complaining to the Immigration

Sugar Estate and Transportation Canal C. 1900

Department against harsh treatment by employers. One planter even boasted that workers on his estate must either be at work, in hospital or in jail during working hours. This meant that workers who finished their job early and went home could be arrested and fined. Those who were discharged from hospital but physically unfit to begin work could also be punished.

Estate managers were able to use the laws to punish workers at will. As a form of intimidation, charges were brought up by managers and then suddenly withdrawn if the workers promised to 'behave themselves' and to pay the cost of the summons. Thus employers could punish workers without even taking them to court. Between 1865 and 1870 of 31,900 cases between managers and indentured workers only a handful were brought against managers. The workers were suspicious of the courts as they believed magistrates 'curried favor' with the planters. As a result, they would take matters in their own hands rather than go to court to seek justice.

The indenture system gave the planters the control which they had wanted since the abolition of slavery. Control provided employers with a regular supply of labor which could be used to lower wages as well. Thus while the profits of the sugar industry were rising, the position of Indians was getting worse. John Jenkins in his revealing book, *The Coolie: His Rights and Wrongs*, described the position of the indentured worker: "He is in the hands of the system which elaborately twists and turns him about, but always leaves him face to face with an impossibility."

Indenture and slavery

There were many similarities between indenture and slavery. Although Indians were often deceived into emigrating, generally they left India more or less voluntarily under contract. Under slavery there was no such contract between master and slaves. Nevertheless, the indentured worker, like the slave, was subject to laws which were made and imposed by the planters. Under both systems the movements of workers were restricted by various laws.

Moreover, both the slave and the indentured worker were made to feel helpless and dependent on the plantation. The right to strike did not exist under both systems.

There were, however, two basic differences between slavery and indenture. The slave was private property and slavery was for life. The indentured worker was an instrument of production and could look forward to his freedom at the end of five years. But the system of reindenture made contracts almost permanent since some immigrants were forced to reindenture for as many as 6 times, or 30 years under contract. Another difference is that the indentured worker received wages while the slave did not. But wages were fixed by the planters and indentured workers could not negotiate for increases. When Chief Justice Joseph Beaumont (1863-1868) described indenture as "a monstrous, rotten system, rooted upon slavery," he clearly knew what he was talking about. The *Times* of London also observed: "... if it be not slavery, [it] is certainly very far from freedom."

Estate drivers

Under indenture the planters continued to use a system which served them so well under slavery -- the driver system. Drivers or *sirdars* were used both as informants and spies. To continue the divide and rule policy, the planters used Indians with some influence as drivers. Drivers were seen as petty tyrants and as a prop to the system. Since drivers allocated the task, they were in a position to reward friends or punish troublemakers. Those who refused to give a bribe or a loan to the driver were penalized. Complaints against drivers often fell on deaf ears as the overseer depended on the report of the driver for the payment of wages.

One outspoken immigrant, Bechu, underlined the power and authority of the estate driver:

The coolies on Plantation Enmore are afraid of being abused
by their drivers, and sometimes struck by them. Of course
these drivers have a certain number of their own men, who
are always on their side, and the coolies are afraid that the

drivers will bring trumped-up charges against them if they were to complain.

Since drivers identified their interests with those of the plantation, they were allowed to set up shops and sell such items as rice, dal, flour, chillies, tobacco and kerosene. In this way the planters were able to tie Indian immigrants to the plantation. At the same time, drivers demanded that immigrants purchased groceries only from their shops. Newly imported workers quickly fell into the clutches of the driver. Those who refused to patronize his shop were punished in the fields with difficult tasks on stiff, clayey soil. The practice of paying workers in a lump sum permitted the driver to deduct sums of money owed by workers for goods supplied on credit.

It was no wonder that conflicts often developed between drivers and other workers. Tension was heightened when the planters placed Black drivers in charge of Indian gangs. During wage disputes workers' anger and frustration often fell on the drivers. Many were beaten and thrown into nearby trenches. At other times, workers would picket the estate for the removal of the driver. The driver system was an essential part of labor control on estates and it has continued to this day.

Wife murders

One of the most criticized aspects of indenture was the alarming number of Indian wife murders in all the sugar colonies. While a shortage of women was a feature in most pioneering societies, the problem in Guyana was allowed to continue for too long. The authorities made little effort to increase the supply of Indian women beyond the required quota of 40 women to every 100 men shipped. Even in the closing years of indenture when the shortage was heavily criticized, little was done to improve the situation. The problem was made worse by the tendency of some European overseers and managers to live with Indian women and the reluctance of Indian men to marry Black women.

The shortage created a grave social problem and was the main reason for the high number of murders of unfaithful wives. It tended to lower the standard of morality in the Indian community. It produced competition for the available number of Indian women and created a feeling of jealousy. As a result, the hoe and the cutlass were used frequently on Indian women. In the period 1859-1864 there were 23 murders of Indian women by their husbands, 11 between 1865 and 1870, 23 between 1884 and 1888 and 17 in the period 1901-1917. Many of these crimes were carried out with such cruelty and barbarity "as to make the blood run cold."

In response to criticism from the British Government and the Government of India, the authorities in Guyana were forced to take action. They called on employers to keep a watchful eye over their work force and to report cases of wives leaving their husbands for other men. Such preventative measures as transferring husbands or seducers to distant estates, and punitive action like hanging and life imprisonment, were also taken. Flogging for men and shaving the heads of women were also suggested as deterrents but were rejected as too cruel. Later the Guyanese Government tried to import Indian widows and betrothed women whose future husbands had died, but without success.

The problems of sexual immorality and polyandry (a woman having several husbands or lovers) thus continued. It was this degraded position of Indian women which gave Indian nationalists vital ammunition to condemn the system and to demand its abolition.

Indian women

In all the importing sugar colonies there was a noticeable shortage of Indian women. This shortage resulted from the fact that there were few unattached women in India because of child betrothal and marriage at an early age. Indians, too, migrated alone as they did not want to subject their wives and children to a searching medical examination for venereal diseases or to the dangers of unknown lands. Despite the payment of higher rates for women recruits, the difficulty of enlisting Indian women in India continued throughout indenture.

Indian women who came to the colonies comprised young widows who found life in India intolerable, and married and single women "who have gone astray" and would not be accepted by their husbands and families. Sometimes, particularly to make up the required quota, prostitutes were shipped from Calcutta. There is, however, no evidence that such women came in any significant number. Very often emigration agents encouraged depot marriages (*sagai*) so as to fill the required quota and keep expenses down.

Indian women were subjected to the same forms of exploitation under the plantation system as men. They had to complete the stated five tasks per week or their pay was docked. Granted that they performed such lighter tasks as weeding and manuring, they were forced to work the same number of hours as the men. Moreover, they received lower wages than male immigrants. Very often nursing mothers were forced to work in the fields under heavy penalty. Circumstances thus forced Indian women to adopt the triple role of mothers, housewives and wage earners.

Estate employers expected Indian women to be placid and submissive. But on the plantations Indian women had shown that they could protest actively as well. As early as the 1870s their militancy on the plantations was noted. In 1872 at Plantation Devonshire Castle on the Essequibo Coast, they stood beside their husbands who were protesting against long working hours and low wages. When ordered to disperse, they refused, waving their fists in a "riotous" manner. A Police Inspector described their behavior when the Riot Act, which gave them an hour to disperse, was read: "During the interval about fifty women came to the front of the strikers, and screamed and cursed in a most diabolical manner. They said they would kill us or die with their husbands."

Very often labor resistance started in the weeding gang where wages were consistently low. Here women in an advanced stage of pregnancy were forced to toil in the fields, a requirement which was bitterly resented. In a major riot at Plantation Friends in Berbice in 1903, a key role was played by a veteran indentured

Working Class Indian Women

was intended to promote fertility among the devotees who hoped to father children. Through a strong campaign of persuasion, the ritual was discontinued in the early 1850s.

The most popular religious observance in the 19th century was Tadjah which commemorated the death of Husain and Hasan, grandsons of the prophet Mohammed. Tadjah was a replica of the tombs of these two brothers. It was carried in a procession and then thrown into running water at the end of the journey. It resembled a pagoda built on a bamboo framework with a height of some 20 feet. It was usually decorated with brightly colored paper and multicolored flags.

Tadjah soon became a national observance in which European sugar planters, Indians, Portuguese, Blacks and Chinese actively participated. It was during this ritual that Indians were able to assert themselves and thus prevent the powerful plantation system from turning them into mere puppets. During the procession, Europeans who failed to dismount from their horse or carriage were often assaulted and thrown into drainage trenches. Fights often broke out when rival Tadjahs clashed in the middle of the road.

As the 19th century progressed, Tadjah lost its significance and took on a carnival style both in Guyana and Trinidad. It was perhaps the popularity of Tadjah with its stick fighting, drumming, dancing, drama and weeping which overshadowed the observation of other Indian rituals in Guyana. As the Tadjah ritual began to wane following criticism by devout Muslims and others, such festivals as Divali, Holi, Kali Mai Puja and Eid became popular in the Guyanese Indian community. In Trinidad, however, the Tadjah observation has continued to this day.

Throughout the indenture period Indian religion was kept alive by the arrival of fresh batches of workers. These new immigrants acted as a link with Village India. The presence of Brahmins and Moulvis who interpreted the scriptures also helped to preserve customs and traditions in the Indian community. The isolation of Indians on the sugar plantations also tended to shield them from Creole practices, though not completely.

Missionary activity

It was assumed among the missionaries in 19th century Guyana that if Indians were free from the control of their priests and from the caste system, their conversion to Christianity would be easier and more lasting. For the job of conversion, priests had to be imported since few in Guyana knew Indian languages. Thus in 1862 E.H. Bose, a Bengali from Calcutta, arrived and was ordained as an Anglican priest. In that same year the Reverend H.V.P. Bronkhurst, an Anglo-Ceylonese, landed and became a Wesleyan Missionary to the Indians. Both men received salaries from the government. To Bose, his main task was to create an Indian church which would function in cooperation with the regular church. Bronkhurst held services in Indian languages but also encouraged Indians to attend the regular Methodist Church.

To convert an estimated 48,976 Indians in 1871 was a huge task. From the outset both missionaries complained of poor results and considerable frustration. Between 1865 and 1870 Bose baptized only 30 Indians. Depressed by his failure to make a greater impact in the Indian community, Bose retired temporarily from the Church in 1870. He then became the official interpreter in Indian languages at court. Bronkhurst, on the other hand, served for 33 years until his death in 1895. Like Bose, his missionary activity met with deep frustration as he was often heckled and jeered by Indians. He found Indians morally and spiritually "as hard as stones and as cold as icicles." In 1872 he wanted to retire but was persuaded to carry on.

Several factors seemed to explain the failure of missionaries to convert Indians to Christianity. Bronkhurst pointed to the Indian aversion "to cast away his own creed for that of strangers." Bose emphasized the strong desire of Indians to return home at the end of their contracts. One Indian expressed this aptly: "Home is home, sweeter than honey and money." There was also the fear that they would be treated as outcasts and shunned by family and friends if they became Christians. Indians also perceived the church as supporters of the planters since missionaries were paid agents of the colony. The practice of integrating Indian Christians into the Black congregations also hindered the spread of the gospel. The increase in rum drinking, lack of teachers acquainted with Indian languages, the long distances between plantations and the isolation of Indians created further obstacles to missionary activity. In the 40 years (1856-1896) a total of 1,163 Indians were converted or an annual average of a mere 29.

The Canadian Presbyterian Mission was established in 1885. It also found the task of conversion difficult, despite the sustained efforts of the Rev. J.B. Cropper who headed it for 40 years (1896-1936). By 1918 only about 10% of those Indians converted to Christianity were members of the Canadian Mission (or Canadian Presbyterians). The popularity of Indian plays, an increase in the building of Mosques and Mandirs and greater Indian participation in religious activities tended to blunt missionary endeavors

Nevertheless, the Presbyterians contributed greatly to lessening the fear of Indian parents to have their children educated in denominational schools. The schools that they built provided employment opportunities for many Indians who were converted to Christianity. Generally, the Presbyterian Mission was more successful than the other missions in converting Indians to Christianity. This was largely because it accommodated many of the preachings of Hinduism and was seen as an Indian church. By 1931 about 6.9% of the Indian population were Christians, 9.2% in 1946.

Christian missionaries lamented the lack of success. What they failed to understand was the resilience of Hinduism and Islam which could adapt and survive in an alien environment. In fact, cultural survival became the most powerful form of resistance against the plantation system. A hundred years after the first Indians arrived, Christianity had made little impact in the Guyanese Indian community.

Superstitious beliefs

Among all peoples superstition or irrational beliefs and fear of the unknown exists. In India, every group in the society has charms for themselves and family, their homes and even their cattle. Superstitious beliefs in the Guyanese Indian community are chiefly associated with pregnancy and birth, love and marriage, death and burial and cures for certain physical ailments. Superstition is also associated with the 'selling' of a child for good health, with starting a journey especially on Friday, launching of a ship or opening a new building, attending a funeral and sneezing. These superstitious beliefs had prevailed since indenture and slavery and had a significant impact on the lives of both Indians and Blacks in Guyana. Today superstition is waning largely because of developments in education and science which enable many Indians to view things rationally and objectively.

Social life

Food
Indians were able to survive on their small weekly income mainly because of their customary diet of rice and curry, so hot that those unaccustomed to it could hardly eat a few spoonfuls. Although fond of mutton, poultry and fish, Hindus refrained from eating beef for religious reasons. The majority of them were vegetarians and the food they were accustomed to could be grown locally or imported in bulk. Hence Indians paid lower import duties on basic consumer items than Creoles who generally adopted European tastes. The isolation of Indians on the plantations helped them to maintain their low cost dietary practices.

Housing
Indians on the plantations lived in *logies* -- old slave barracks which were cramped and poorly ventilated. In 1929 Andrews described the poor condition of the *logies* at Plantation Skeldon:

Indian Women Bedecked With Jewelry

41

"Some of them must be fifty years old; and the filth that has been continually thrown outside the door (where no drain exists at all) must have accumulated in such layers that the ground in front of the lines were almost like a cesspit."

Some Indians built their own homes on estate land with building materials provided by estate managers either free of cost or at a small fee. The walls of these cottages were covered with clay and the clay floors daubed with cow dung to provide a smooth surface. These dwellings were simple with hardly any furniture. Some Indians slept on *katiyas* (cots made with ropes tied together); others, on mats made of coconut leaves. These cottages reminded officials very much of Mother India "with its mud-walled and thatched houses of the natives." From the late 1950s the *logies* began to disappear as sugar workers were given loans to build their own homes on extra-nuclear housing schemes developed by the estates.

Dress

In this colonial society English mode of dress (pants, jacket, tie) predominated. The coming of Indians led to the introduction of a different mode of dress. During most of the 19th century Indian men wore the kurta and dhoti or baba which left parts of their bodies exposed. It was this style of dress which led the British to describe Gandhi as the "naked fakir." Such mode of dress was often found "indecent" by other groups which called on government to compel Indian men to wear a short underpants from the waist to the knee. The *sirdar* usually dressed differently from the rest of the gang.

Indian women wore multicolored saris or full skirts, colorful *julas* (bodices) and *ornis* (veils). Many were adorned with an assortment of gold and silver jewelry -- nose rings, necklaces, bangles, foot rings, bracelets and amulets. These made music as the women moved about. Visitors were often amazed at the amount of jewelry worn by Indian women. Such display of apparent wealth often excited the envy of the Blacks.

Music

Indians who landed in Guyana and other parts of the Caribbean came from a rich folk culture. They brought their customs and traditions, the music of their villages and the songs of their festivals and religious ceremonies. Their folk musical instruments included the *Dholak, Tassa, Sarangi, Dand-tal* and *Harmonium*, and the folk theatre was a medium through which their music, dance and dramas were preserved. The most popular folk dances/songs were the *Nagara* or Ahir dance, the *Beeraha* and the *Jhumar*. Indian folk music kept them in touch with their history and culture. It also tended to provide a sense of identity and to prevent the plantation from completely dominating their lives.

Music also seemed to provide relief and comfort from the harsh, boring plantation life. On evenings Indians would read from the Koran or from the Hindu scriptures, sing *Bhajans* or chant from the *Ramayana*. Gradually folk songs developed for different occasions; for rice planting and harvesting, the grinding of grains and lulling children to sleep. There were also songs to comfort lonely women whose husbands were working far from home. Music also played an important part during Holi (when *chowtals* were sung) and Divali celebrations. The drumming and singing during the Tadjah procession provided perhaps the best evidence of the rhythm of Indian music. Today a blend of chutney and soca with Hindi film music is part and parcel of Indian music in the Caribbean.

Language

Coming from different parts of India, Indians introduced their own native languages which have largely disappeared except in religious ceremonies. Hindus spoke Hindi, Bhojpuri and other languages and soon Hindi became the main language in the Indian community. By the end of indenture at least 75% of Indians in Guyana spoke Hindi or a Hindi dialect and about 5% Tamil. Muslims who then comprised about 16 % of the total number of Indians spoke Hindustani, a mixture of Hindi and Urdu. These languages did not survive because of the predominance of the English language, the shortage of Indian teachers and limited funding by the government. Indian parents who decided to set up permanent homes in Guyana recognized the advantage of an English education for professional advancement in the society. Knowledge of the English language was also important to enter politics.

Caste

The castes of Indians represented largely those found in the villages in India. In Guyana and other sugar colonies, the lower agricultural castes (chamars, dosadhs and others) were in the majority. Other numerically important groups were from the cultivator caste (kurmis, lodhs, jats), the grazier caste (ahirs, goalas), the landholding and military caste (kshatriyas, thakurs), the artisan caste (kumhars, koris) and priestly and intellectual caste (brahmins).

In an examination of the castes of Indians in Guyana (from the emigration certificates) between the years 1865 and 1917, Raymond Smith, a sociologist, found that Brahmins and other high castes comprised 13.6 %, agricultural castes 30.1 %, artisans 8.7 %, low castes and outcasts 31.1 %, Muslims 16.3 % and Christians 0.1 %. These numbers, however, may not reflect the true position since immigrants often falsified their caste to start afresh in a new land. Some (often referred to as 'ship Brahmins') assumed high caste status during the voyage with the hope of getting a good job in the colonies.

Caste distinctions became very difficult to keep up. The cramped conditions in the depot, on the voyage overseas and in the *logies* forced high castes to mingle with low castes. Inter-caste marriages were often the result of such intermingling. D.W.D. Comins, Protector of Emigrants at Calcutta, visited Guyana in 1891 and found little evidence of caste distinctions. He reported marriages between high and low castes and between Hindus and Muslims.

The caste system was also weakened by employers allotting work without regard to caste. Very often low caste drivers were put in charge of high caste immigrants. The weakening of caste, however, helped Indians to take up different occupations which the caste system in India did not permit. Such occupations included jewelry making, carpentry, tailoring and barbering (hair cutting).

Some Indians, too, tried to move up the social ladder by assuming English names. One early example was Gunapathy Pillai who changed his name to Samuel Johnson. He landed in Guyana as an indentured worker in 1848 and 4 years later became an interpreter in the Immigration Department. After serving for 27 years, he rose to one of the highest positions in that office. Other names that were changed closely resembled English ones, for example, Suleiman became Solomon.

Family Life

The Indian ideal of family life stresses the importance of the extended family. The extended family is headed by the father or, in his absence, the elder brother. After marriage the daughter-in-law becomes part of the family. Every member helps to run the household and to build up the resources of the family. The uncles and other relatives are also concerned with the welfare of the family and try to help in whatever way they can. All relatives are addressed in the traditional Indian way, e.g. *chacha* for uncle. This system produces a sort of unity and cooperative spirit within the household and ensures progress in agriculture.

In Guyana this family system tended to survive particularly in rice-growing areas where sons might continue to live in the same household after marriage. But after a few years it was normal for sons to be provided with a house and some land to farm. The extended family might also continue for some time where heavy population and housing shortage tended to prevent sons from branching out on their own. A joint business venture might also preserve the extended family for some time.

On the estate a modified form of the extended family system existed but several factors helped to undermine the system. The position of the father as head of the household was weakened as estate managers gave equal recognition to all workers. Estate houses were also provided to working, married sons which made them independent of their father. Moreover, tension between a young wife and her mother-in-law often led the wife to persuade her husband to break away from the family.

There were other factors as well. The small proportion of Indian women to men made it difficult to establish a stable family life. The fact that Indians came as individuals, not as family groups, tended to undermine the extended family. Indian children who received an English education often tended to separate from their families. The breaking down of the arranged marriage system also threatened the extended family system.

In time the extended family was replaced by the nuclear family (man, wife and children). Nevertheless, although living apart, married sons tend to keep constant contact with the family and share the responsibility of seeing that the other children are married. It was commitment to the family which facilitated thrift and industry among Indians.

Occupation

Up to the early 1890s the skilled jobs (blacksmiths, mechanics, carpenters, engineers) in the building or factory were in the hands of Black workers. In the fields they also specialized in such high paid jobs as shoveling (digging of drains and canals) and canecutting. With the discovery of gold in the Essequibo in the 1880s, many Black workers quit the sugar estates for the mines where the opportunity for wealth accumulation seemed unlimited.

Thus by the late 1890s some Indians were beginning to move into the skilled jobs both in the field and factory. Some could even match the stalwart Black worker in handling the shovel. The majority of Indians, however, were employed in such unskilled

Indian Canecutters in the 1890s

jobs as weeding, manuring, hoeing, cane replanting, grass cutting and trench clearing.

Employment of women and children was a part of estate life. Children were employed largely to tend estate cattle; women, as grass cutters, weeders and cane manurers. The 1891 Census showed that a large number of Indian children under the age of 15 were employed in estate agriculture.

Free Indians (those who completed their contracts) living on the estates took up different occupations. One was huckstering, selling such articles as tobacco, potatoes, flour, rice and dal to estate immigrants and to Blacks and Indians in the neighboring villages. Another occupation was cattle rearing and milk selling. Free Indians quickly dominated the milk trade which became a very profitable business. Sometimes milk sellers were caught diluting their milk with rain or trench water. Money lending at high interest rates, jewelry making, fortune telling and baptizing of Indian children also enabled some Indians to acquire a small fortune. Fortune telling was popular particularly among Indian women who desired to know their destiny.

It was estimated in 1891 that 35,668 free Indians out of an Indian population of 107,439 were living off the estates and they took up a variety of occupations. A government report listed them as follows:

> rice cultivation, cattle farming, growing provisions, jobbers about town, grass-cutters, gardeners, grooms, jockeys, fishermen, cabmen, cartmen, milk sellers, tramcar drivers, hucksters, merchants, mechanics, clerks, barbers, boatmen, tailors, rope-makers, charcoal burners, goldsmiths, workers in clay, domestic servants, manufacturers of coconut oil, sweetmeats vendors, boxwallahs [peddlers], bakers, chemists, shop-keepers.

By the first quarter of the 20th century there were 238 Indian jewelers, 445 shopkeepers, 845 hucksters, 259 milk sellers, 12,465 rice farmers and 13,700 landed proprietors, agriculturists and cattle farmers.

Indian village settlements

During the latter part of the 19th century the formation of Indian village settlements was frowned upon by the planters. They believed that the acquisition of land by Indians would provide a measure of independence and this would weaken their control over labor. It was the high cost of repatriating time-expired Indians (those who completed their contracts and were entitled to a free return passage to India) which forced the planters to give serious thought to the establishment of Indian settlements. It was estimated in 1869 that 30,000 Indians were entitled to a free return passage to India at a total cost of $250,000. By 1880 the number of Indians who could claim a free return passage had doubled.

To avoid this huge liability, the planters took action to create land settlement schemes. In 1871 the government bought Plantation Nooten Zuill, an abandoned 578 acre cattle and provision farm on the East Coast Demerara, to settle time-expired Indians. It was proposed to settle 225 Indians, each having one-half acre lot to build a house, one and a half acre for farming and one-half acre for cattle grazing on common pasturage. A legally married couple would receive double the acreage for farming and grazing rights. The scheme failed largely because of poor drainage, inadequate land for pasture and the small size of the grants. By January 1875 no allotments were accepted and the estate was sold to a neighboring proprietor at a loss.

In 1880 the high cost of repatriation led the government to purchase Plantation Huist t' Dieren on the Essequibo to form another settlement. This experiment met with limited success. Between 1896 and 1902 four more settlements -- Helena, Whim, Bush Lot and Maria's Pleasure -- were bought, prepared and allotted to immigrants in lieu of a return passage. Altogether 1206 settlers bought lots of one-fifth of an acre at Helena, 574 at Whim, 755 at Bush Lot and 176 at Maria's Pleasure.

By 1902 the government stopped experimenting with Indian villages for various reasons. First, from 1905 male returnees had to contribute one-half and females one-third of their return passage costs. Consequently, the planters' liability for providing return passages was reduced considerably. Second, the planters claimed that the villages failed because many residents refused to pay the rates and did not live on their lots. Thirdly and most importantly, the planters were not prepared to incur expenses which would exceed the cost of sending Indians back to India. When they realized that few Indians would contribute towards the passage costs and thus return home, they abandoned the village experiment. The planters were concerned more with their selfish interests than with the success of the villages.

Return passage

When the first batch of Indians arrived in Guyana, their contracts stated that they would be provided with a free return passage to India at the end of five years. Since this was the first experiment with Indian labor in the Caribbean, the British Government wanted to ensure that a free return passage was guaranteed.

With the reopening of Indian immigration, the sugar planters wanted longer contracts, instead of the existing monthly contracts, or a contribution by immigrants towards the return passage. Following a long campaign, the planters got what they wanted. From 1854 Indians would be indentured for 5 years but would be only entitled to a free return passage after 10 years. This meant that they had to reindenture for another period of 5 years.

As immigration progressed, the planters tried to get rid of the return passage entitlement altogether. In the 1850s they urged the British Government to approve a policy whereby Indians would give up their right to return home in exchange for suitable grants of land. Realizing that the generally uneducated Indians could be deceived, the Government of India proposed the appointment of an Indian official as Protector of Immigrants to safeguard their interests. This proposal was rejected by the British Government and the scheme was dropped. The British Government feared that such an appointment might lead to conflicts between the Indian official and local officers.

In 1875 the planters again called for the abolition of the return passage entitlement. They argued that the entitlement not only increased immigration costs but resulted in the loss of experienced workers. They questioned the wisdom of sending back such workers to India where they could barely subsist or starve during famines. The Government of India, however, refused the request. It claimed that the entitlement was the only protection Indians had against harsh treatment in the sugar colonies. Moreover, it argued that the withdrawal of the entitlement would result in fewer Indians leaving their villages for employment overseas. A few years later the Indian Government rejected another request for abolition.

During the depression in the sugar industry in the 1890s, the planters again called on the British Government to relieve them of the return passage liability. They argued that if the sugar industry collapsed, immigration would be stopped and thousands of indentured workers would be out of work. This time the Government of India was forced to make some concession. It agreed that in future, male emigrants would contribute one-half ($30) and females one-third ($20) towards their own passage costs. In 1902 the planters again called for total abolition but again the request was rejected. When indenture ended, the entitlement remained an important part of the contract.

Since the mid-1840s the planters had conducted a strong campaign against the granting of a free return passage. Although the Government of India made some concession, it never gave up the entitlement which was considered the binding link to India. In 1938 a change of policy occurred. Now the planters were taking steps to repatriate Indians amid protests from the Government of India that they should remain in the colonies and set up permanent homes. The Indian Government had adopted this new policy because of the serious adjustment problems returning emigrants faced on arrival in India. The planters nevertheless, continued to provide a return passage to India. The last two steamships to repatriate Guyanese Indians were the *Orna* (1949) which carried 311 passengers and the *Resurgent* (1955) some 245.

Education

In the early phase of immigration the Indian community took little interest in an English education. In 1901 about 80% of Indian children did not attend school; 75% in 1913. In 1923 while about 71% of Indian children were not attending school, among the Chinese it was 17%, Blacks or Coloreds 21%, Portuguese 25% and Amerindians 59%.

There were several reasons for the general lack of education in English in the Indian community. The Compulsory Education Act of 1876, which required mandatory attendance at school, was applied more strictly to the urban areas than to the rural areas where the majority of Indians lived. There were also more schools and greater educational facilities in the urban areas of Georgetown and New Amsterdam. Moreover, most estates cut expenses by employing children under the age of 12 years. A large number of children were thus sent to work to supplement the family income. The small number of Indian teachers (104 out of 1455 in 1929) must have contributed to the low enrollment of Indian children. In addition, since girls could be married at 13 (changed to 14 in 1929) many parents saw no benefit from a few years of schooling.

Indian parents, too, had different attitudes towards an English education for their children. Many objected to the existing system which combined education with Christianity as most of the schools were denominational or church-controlled schools. The various denominations (Canadian Mission, Roman Catholic, Wesleyan, Moravian and Baptist) owned and managed the schools while government paid the salaries of teachers and met other expenses. Many parents preferred to allow their children to "grow up in ignorance" than to be converted to Christianity or taught by Black teachers. Those who wished to return to India saw no benefit in educating their children in English.

On the other hand, the children of prosperous Indians who lived in the urban areas enjoyed the best educational facilities. It was from this middle-class group that prominent educated Indians (Luckhoos, Jacobs, Ruhomans) emerged.

The Swettenham Circular, issued by Governor James Swettenham in 1902, was perhaps the biggest obstacle to the education of Indian children. The Circular instructed that during the first decade after arrival, Indian parents would not be penalized for disobeying the education act. After that period, they could still ignore the law if they objected to an English education on religious grounds. Furthermore, parents who refused to allow their daughters to attend school could be exempt from punishment.

The Circular certainly prevented the development of a literate Indian population for it kept children in the fields where child labor performed important estate services. It was the withdrawal of the Circular in 1933 which opened the way for the education of Indian girls. By this time Indians had fully realized the importance of learning English to obtain a good job. Between 1933 and 1937 East Indian enrollment in the primary schools had increased by nearly 50%. By 1946 roughly 56% of Indians were literate.

Politics

As in education, Indians showed little interest in politics throughout the indenture period. Although in 1917 Indians formed 57.8% of the adult male population of voting age, less than 1% were registered as voters. By 1925 while comprising over 40% of the colony's total population, the Indian community in Guyana formed only 13% of the registered voters.

There were several reasons for the lack of Indian participation in the electoral process. First, from the time Guyana became a British colony, both political and economic power were in the hands of the planting and mercantile interests, and this situation continued to independence. They ensured that all other interests remained secondary to those of sugar. Second, up to the early 1930s the interests of Indians in the local legislature were guarded by the Immigration Agent-General. Since this officer had the responsibility of investigating grievances and settling disputes, Indians had little incentive to enter politics. Third, the main concern of Indians was to build a strong economic base, to return to India to pay off debts and reclaim their lands. Fourth, Indians generally had little knowledge of the English language and this prevented them from entering politics. Fifthly, there was a noticeable absence of Indian leaders who could muster Indians into a political force. It was not until the 1930s and 40s that elected Indians began to enter the local legislature.

Impact of indenture

Life under the indenture system was very harsh as Indians found themselves in a helpless situation. For the first 30 years under indenture they were treated as criminals, even for minor offenses, and prevented from giving evidence at court on their own behalf. Indians believed that they could not get justice at court because magistrates tended to sleep at the homes of the planters before attending court the next morning. Thus Indians had no confidence in the courts because they believed that the decisions of Magistrates were biased.

For nearly a century the minimum wage of 25 cents a day remained unchanged while the cost of living continued to rise. When the wages of workers were stopped, there was no provision in the law for them to recover such wages. If they went on strike, they could be arrested, fined, imprisoned or transferred to distant estates. The indentured Indians were thus at the mercy of the planters as Beaumont observed:

> Practically an Immigrant is in the hands of the employer to whom he is bound; he cannot live without work; he can only get such work and on such terms as the employer chooses to set him and all these necessities are enforced ... by the terrors of imprisonment and the prospect of losing both favour and wages.

Thus Indians were overworked and underpaid. They were often beaten by estate drivers or their henchmen if they protested against low wages or long working hours. Those who spoke on their behalf were either dismissed or stripped of their powers.

James Crosby

There was, however, one agency which was legally set up in 1839 to help Indians -- the Immigration Department headed by the Immigration Agent-General. It was this officer who had the important task of ensuring that the welfare of Indians was protected and that employers carried out their legal responsibilities. The longest serving Protector of Indians in all the sugar colonies was Crosby. He held the post of Immigration Agent-General from 1858 to his death in 1880 at the age of 74. He performed his duties so ably and diligently that the office became popularly known as 'Crosby Office'.

In Crosby Indians found a genuine friend and a champion of their rights. They would take their complaints to him with full confidence that investigations would be made and their problems remedied. The duties of Crosby included visiting immigrant ships, inspecting immigrants on arrival, prosecuting employers at court and dealing with the estates of deceased immigrants. Crosby also had the power to enter sugar estates at any time to examine pay lists and to inspect hospital accommodation and housing conditions.

For the first few years Crosby had complete control over the affairs of the Immigration Department. However, from 1864 serious disagreements arose between him and the "scheming", energetic Governor Francis Hincks. The conflict with the proplanter Hincks stemmed from Crosby's prosecution of employers who illtreated immigrants. Consequently, Hincks denied Crosby the customary travel allowances which prevented him from visiting estates and listening to workers' complaints. Then Hincks took measures to deprive Crosby of all independent action. Crosby could only act with the expressed approval of Hincks. As a result,

Crosby could not take employers to court for illtreating or underpaying workers. This duty was transferred to the police who hardly acted to redress the complaints of workers.

Two other officials, Beaumont and Stipendiary Magistrate William Des Voeux, also tried to protect the welfare of Indians but were muzzled. Beaumont was accused of judicial misconduct and, following a plot by Hincks and the business community to remove him from office, he was dismissed as Chief Justice. Des Voeux was forced to accept an appointment in another colony at a reduced salary. Indians were thus left at the mercy of employers. For them to survive, they would have to take matters in their own hands.

Labor disturbances

Beginning from the late 1860s a number of strikes and labor demonstrations occurred in the sugar belt. Several explanations for these strikes were given. The planters argued that Brahmins and ex-sepoys were instigating workers to strike. Others believed that workers were becoming more assertive as they realized that an official commission was investigating labor conditions in the colony. But the main explanation was that most workers were seasoned hands who were prepared to protest when wages fell below the minimum rate.

The first strike began at Leonora in July 1869 when 40 workers of the shovel gang complained that their wages were withheld for unfinished work. The following year violence flared up at Plantations Hague, Uitvlugt, Mon Repos, Non Pareil, Zeelugt, Vergenoegen and Success. The most serious conflict in the 1870s occurred at Plantation Devonshire Castle on the Essequibo Coast where five Indians -- Maxidally, Beccaroo, Kaulica, Baldeo and Ackloo -- were shot and killed by the police. These were the first Indians to lose their lives while fighting against injustice and planter exploitation.

Throughout the last quarter of the 19th century clashes between the police and sugar workers occurred on a regular basis. Most centered on low wages and long working hours. One very serious confrontation took place at Non Pareil in October 1896, resulting in the death of five Indians from buck shots. Although a reduction in wages was the main cause of the strike, there was considerable anger among Indians over the fact that Acting Manager, Gerad Van Nooten, was living with an Indian woman. In the clash with the police, the woman's husband, Jungli, was among those who died.

In the 20th century, up to 1938, there were five main confrontations between the police and sugar workers. In 1903 the attempt by the manager at Friends in Berbice to reduce wages for 'half banking' work (preparing the rows for the replanting of cane tops) resulted in a clash with the police and the death of six Indians.

The most violent clash between Indian workers and the police in the indenture period took place at Plantation Rose Hall, Berbice, in 1913. On this plantation Indians had several grievances. They were peeved over the excessively long hours of work with no extra pay, the high rents charged for rice beds and the bullying attitude of the manager and the head driver, Jugmohan. Tension mounted when the manager suddenly withdrew his promise to grant workers four days holiday in addition to those prescribed by law. When the workers protested, the manager ordered the arrest and transfer of the 'ring leaders' and their spouses to distant estates. In the confrontation with the police, 15 Indians were shot and killed including an indentured woman, Gobindei. The shooting was condemned in India and elsewhere and it certainly helped the campaign to abolish the system.

Between 1917 and 1939 major clashes between the police and the sugar workers occurred at Plantation Ruimveldt and at Leonora. The troubles at Ruimveldt originated in a dispute over rates of pay for dock workers in Georgetown. Tension spilled over into the plantations on the East Bank Demerara where estate personnel were assaulted. On 3 April, 1924 a large crowd of Indians and Blacks from the East Bank "began its march on Georgetown." They were stopped at Ruimveldt to prevent their entry into the city. In the struggle the police shot and killed 13 and arrested 77. What was significant about this riot was that sugar workers, both Indians and Blacks, appeared united in their fight against oppression.

In the 1930s dissatisfaction leading to riots was widespread in Guyana, Barbados, Trinidad , Jamaica and the Windward and Leeward Islands. It followed a financial crisis in New York which spread to other parts of the world including the Caribbean. The last of these riots took place in February 1939 at Leonora, an estate which had a history of workers' resistance. Without reading the Riot Act, as they should, the police fired on the 'ring leaders' killing four workers including Sumintra, a young female weeder.

The Leonora strike was significant. It forced the sugar producers to grant recognition to the Man Power Citizens Association (MPCA), a recently formed trade union headed by Ayube Eden, a goldsmith by trade. For the first time in a hundred years a trade union was formed in Guyana to represent solely the interests of sugar workers, one of the most exploited groups in the history of the working class movement in Guyana.

In the hundred years, 1838-1938, over 600 strikes and 50 deaths were recorded on the sugar estates in Guyana. These strikes, which resulted in assaults on managers, drivers and overseers, tended to destroy and put to rest the notion that Indians were a docile people. They showed that Indians were capable of taking appropriate action when pressed too far. The British in India had realized this only too well during the Sepoy Mutiny of 1857. Although the police often used a heavy hand to put down these strikes, their presence did not deter Indians from protesting against tyranny and oppression. Very often Indian sugar workers were 'knocked down' but they were never 'knocked out'.

Indian leadership

During these periods of unrest Indian workers suffered from a lack of leaders to channel their protests or air their grievances. Besides Bechu, who criticized the abuses of the indenture system in the local press, no identifiable leader emerged from within the ranks of the work force. It was only in the late 1930s with the birth of the MPCA that a few leaders, mostly merchants and businessmen, were identified. Cheddi Jagan who left an indelible imprint on the politics of the region emerged in the late 1940s.

There were several reasons for the lack of leadership in the Guyanese Indian community. The majority of Indians were drawn from the lower agricultural and laboring castes and were being introduced into an environment which was alien to them. Many had little knowledge of life beyond the narrow confines of their villages. The system of indenture, too, was geared to stifle leadership and to make workers helpless and dependent on the planters. Through the 'pass' system their movements were confined to the plantation and they were subjected to heavy penalty for breaches of the law. Indians whose indentures were coming to an end wanted to risk nothing which would delay their freedom or their return passage entitlement. Indians who were inclined to speak out against injustice were threatened and punished by drivers and their henchmen. Heavy fines, quick arrest and imprisonment of 'ring leaders', threats of eviction and transfers to distant estates were all intended to stifle leadership in the Indian community.

Moreover, those who could provide leadership were co-opted into the system as drivers or headmen. Other potential leaders like Brahmins and 'returnees' (those who remigrated after claiming a return passage) were debarred from entering Guyana. In fact, from the early 1870s the Emigration Agent at Calcutta was instructed not to enlist these workers as they allegedly helped to ferment unrest on estates. Without capable leaders, Indian workers found it difficult to voice their grievances.

Bechu

Despite the many obstacles to the emergence of Indian leadership, one fearless fighter, Bechu, carried out a sustained attack on the indenture system. Bechu was the only indentured worker to submit a memorandum and testify before the 1898 West India Royal Commission which investigated the problems in the sugar industry. Bechu, a *kurmi* (laboring caste) from Calcutta, landed in Guyana in 1896 at the age of 36 and was indentured to Enmore, East Coast Demerara. He lost his parents at an early age but seemed to have received a good education from "a white lady missionary." Bechu found canecutting physically taxing and was given domestic duties at the manager's house. He used every opportunity to read and thus seemed to have a thorough knowledge of the indenture system and the plight of the indentured workers on estates.

In his letters to the local press and in his memorandum and evidence before the 1898 Commission, Bechu condemned various aspects of the indenture system. He attacked the long hours of labor in the fields, the frequent wage deductions from workers' pay packets and the use of task work to coerce indentured workers. Bechu exposed the tyranny of estate drivers who used their henchmen to threaten and silence those who complained. He claimed that the Immigration Department had abandoned its role of protecting indentured Indians: "The immigration agent [at Enmore] comes round once a month, he is only there for about an hour, and during that time all the coolies are in the field."

In his memorandum Bechu denounced the immoral sexual relations between estate personnel and Indian women. He alleged that it was "an open secret" that white overseers were "keeping" Indian women on several estates. He cited, for example, the case of a Punjabi who wanted to marry Lello, an indentured woman. The man was forced to abandon his plans when he learned that the woman was "in tow" with an overseer who gave her money to buy her freedom. Such connection often produced discontent and resentment leading to riots on estates. The riots at Non Pareil in 1896 stemmed directly from an affair between a married Indian woman and the estate manager.

Bechu also highlighted the tragic case of an indentured Indian, Bhagri, who died after being turned away from the estate hospital. This spirited Indian worker accused Frederick Bascom, manager of Plantation Cove and John, of discharging Bhagri from the hospital while he was sick and without the knowledge or permission of the estate doctor. Bhagri died shortly afterwards.

In an effort to silence Bechu, the authorities charged him with libel and even thought of deporting him to India. Bechu was tried twice but the sources seemed to be silent on the outcome of the case or his activities thereafter. What was certain was that Bechu's allegations could produce unrest in the Indian community and criticism in India. This was a situation which the planters were not prepared to tolerate. In fact, all those who criticized the indenture system or championed the rights of workers paid a heavy price.

Indian Government policy

Throughout the indenture period the Government of India adopted a neutral position towards emigration overseas. It tried to ensure that Indians were enlisted by licensed recruiters, that they knew their destination and understood the terms of their contracts. It took measures to ensure safety and comfort on the voyage and to keep mortality to a minimum. It expected that in the colonies the planters would treat workers justly and provide them with a free return passage to India at the end of their contracts. Once the Government of India was satisfied that these conditions were being fulfilled, it was prepared to allow the planting interests to recruit workers in India.

This policy of benevolent neutrality was maintained for over 70 years. It was not until Gandhi called attention to racial discrimination against Indians in South Africa that a change of policy occurred. When the government of Natal refused to withdraw certain discriminatory laws against Indian traders, the Government of India took action to stop emigration to any country where Indians were not treated fairly. Thus in 1911 Indian emigration to Natal was stopped. The following year Gopal Krishna Gokhale, a leading Indian nationalist, called for the total abolition of indenture. Although his motion in the Indian Legislative Council was defeated, it gave warning that the abolition issue would not go away.

Abolition of indenture

Between 1912 and 1917 a strong campaign against indenture was mounted in India by several organizations and prominent individuals. The campaign was similar to the Antislavery movement in England a century earlier. Organizations such as the Indentured Coolie Protection Society and the *Marwari Sahayak Samiti* warned villagers against emigration and distributed anti-indenture leaflets in several districts of northern India. These pamphlets warned that emigrants would be treated as criminals in the colonies and denied food and wages. Indian women organizations, political parties (the Indian National Congress and the Muslim League) and Indian newspapers also condemned the system. Andrews called for total abolition because he believed the system was "legalized slavery."

But it was Lord Hardinge, Viceroy of India (1910-1916), who produced the most damaging charges against indenture. Hardinge condemned the fraudulent recruiting system, the high suicide rate, the shortage of Indian women and the high number of court prosecutions against indentured Indians. He pointed out that the system no longer benefited Indians who could earn similar wages in India without the risk of losing caste. He believed that indenture degraded Indians and that it was a blot on the *izzat* (honor) of India. Coming from such an important official, these criticisms certainly helped the anti-indenture campaign.

The belief that Indian women were leading immoral lives in the colonies shocked an Indian public that put great store on the chastity of their women folk. And so in response to sustained criticism and the need for Indian labor in the World War I campaigns in Europe, the British Government suspended Indian immigration in 1917. Three years later the system officially came to an end.

Colonization Scheme

The decision to abolish indenture led the Government of India and the British Government to frame an alternative labor scheme. In the Caribbean an intercolonial conference, comprising representatives from Guyana, Trinidad and Jamaica, met in Port-of-Spain (Trinidad) to examine the impact of abolition and to decide on the future policy on immigration. They agreed that Indian immigration was vital to the region and devised a scheme which was similar to indenture. Later in London, a new scheme was framed to encourage land settlement following a three year term of employment on the estates.

When the scheme was announced in India, it was heavily criticized. Motilall Nehru, (father of then India's future Prime Minister, Jawaharlal Nehru), and others claimed that it was "regulated serfdom." Due to widespread opposition, the Government of India was reluctant to approve the scheme. Besides, both Trinidad and Jamaica found the cost of financing the scheme too high and opted out.

Nevertheless, Guyana continued to pursue the Colonization Scheme. The authorities sent out a deputation headed by J.J. Nunan (Attorney General) and J.A. Luckhoo (Barrister-at-Law) to India. They visited India twice and discussed the terms with several Indian leaders. This was followed by visits to Guyana by the Bahadur Pillai/V.N. Tivary delegation in 1922, and three years later by Kunwar Maharaj Singh, an Indian Government official.

The scheme never got off the ground. Besides opposition from Gandhi, there were protests against the scheme in various parts of India. The high cost of implementing the scheme, and opposition from Black leaders in Guyana who feared the loss of political power from the introduction of more Indians, also ensured its demise. Besides, some local Indian leaders were against the venture. The scheme was thus stifled at birth.

Indian representation

By the 1930s Indians formed over 42% of the total Guyanese population but less than 20% of the electorate (those who were eligible to vote). They were also underrepresented in the teaching, police and civil services. It was largely the need to voice the interests of Indians that the British Guiana East Indian Association (BGEIA) was formed in 1916. It owed its origin to Joseph Ruhoman, brother of Guyanese author Peter Ruhoman, who was among the first group of Indo-Guyanese intellectuals. He criticized the intellectual backwardness of Indians and their lack of representation in government and called for positive efforts to improve their lot.

The planks in the platform of the BGEIA included the creation of land settlement schemes for time-expired Indians, the establishment of government schools, the appointment of more Indians in the civil service and the enforcement of the education act for Indian children. The BGEIA also called for a change in the constitution so that Indians who could read and write in their own languages were eligible to vote.

In the mid-1930s the BGEIA passed a number of resolutions on behalf of Indians. These resolutions stemmed from the Census of 1931 which showed that less than 1% of Indians were in the civil service and less than 7% in the teaching service. Consequently, the BGEIA called on the Guyanese Government to minimize illiteracy among the Indian adult population, to reserve a number of places in the Teachers' Training Center for Indians and to employ more Indians in the civil service. The organization alleged that Indians were being discriminated against as preference in the civil service was given to other groups in the proportion of six to one Indian.

The British Government rejected these resolutions. It claimed that there was no racial discrimination in the country and that appointments in the civil service must be based on merit rather than special representation. Thus Indian underrepresentation continued and today it is still noticeable, particularly in the security forces and in the civil service.

The BGEIA highlighted the plight of Indians but it did not achieve much. The organization had little appeal to sugar workers as its activities were mainly confined to Georgetown. Moreover, the merchants and shopkeepers who took control of the organization were more interested in religious and cultural activities than in politics. Nevertheless, the BGEIA had succeeded in awakening Indians politically by bringing issues affecting them into national politics.

Race relations

Throughout the indenture period the relations between Indians and Blacks was described as neither friendly nor hostile. From the 1840s both groups were separated at work and place of residence. The Blacks had the high-paying skilled jobs while Indians largely did unskilled work. The Blacks lived mainly in villages or in the urban areas while Indians were isolated on the plantations. There was thus little competition for jobs, housing and women.

Nevertheless, tension did exist between them. The Blacks believed that Indians were imported to create competition for jobs and to reduce wages. The planters also exploited the tension between the two groups to preserve their power. On many occasions they used Blacks against Indians when violence broke out on the plantations. Some planters, too, put Black drivers in charge of Indian gangs. Many of these drivers were often reported for their bullying attitude towards Indians. In the 1870s the local press reported several cases of Black drivers assaulting Indian indentured workers. It was possible that clashes between the two groups were more widespread since many were localized and were not reported.

Racial tension seemed to increase from the late 1890s. By this time Indians were moving into jobs which were once dominated by the Blacks. The Blacks showed their resentment against the Indian presence in two petitions to the British Government -- one in 1873 and another in 1903. They claimed that Indian immigration was cheapening the work force and throwing thousands out of jobs.

Street – Scene in Georgetown in 1888
Showing the Mix of Blacks and Indians

They argued that it was unfair to use taxpayers' money to finance immigration and to support sick and aged Indians in public institutions. Moreover, they objected to the hoarding of money by some Indians. They attacked the Indian practice of melting down silver coins to make jewelry and their habits of sending money back to India. Even the dress of Indians was criticized. The bottom line of their arguments was that Indian immigration had served its purpose and should be discontinued.

The most serious racial conflict in the indenture period occurred in 1913 at Plantation De Kinderen on the East Coast Demerara. It involved a large number of Indians (Punjabis) and Blacks from the surrounding areas. The conflict began in a dispute between Harilall, an Indian laborer, and a Black peddler, Weeks, over the price of a mirror. As they haggled over the price, Weeks lost his temper and struck Harilall who retaliated. Fortunately, the police intervened to prevent a possible bloody confrontation between the two groups. Following two days of tension, and the arrest and imprisonment of a few Indians and Blacks, the riots subsided.

At times Indians were forced to defend themselves against criticism and verbal abuse. During the mid-1840s a large number of Indians came from the Madras Presidency. They were mockingly referred to as 'sammy' because many of their names ended in 'sammy' or 'sawmy' (Ramasawmy, Kandasammy, Motoosammy). Later 'sammy' was replaced by the degrading term 'coolie' which is still in use today. S. Mohamed Baksh, a regular correspondent in the *Argosy*, voiced the Indian resentment against this derogatory term:

Coolies are labourers such as work on sugar estates or do odd jobs about town. But take a walk anywhere in the colony and you will find East Indians in positions other than these. See how farmers work planting rice, and cleaning and making paddy into rice. If there is ever to be any opening up of the country, it is to the East Indian you must look, as he is gradually occupying the available lands for farming.

In 1929 Andrews called attention to the tension between Indians and Blacks: "... an undercurrent of something which might be called rivalry or even jealousy between the two communities wherever they live side by side." Andrews believed that as Indians took advantage of education and demanded more representation in the teaching profession and civil service, interracial conflicts would increase. They did flare up in the early 1960s when Guyanese witnessed the bloodiest racial confrontation in their history.

Social and economic conditions

Social

Reports from Indian Government officials, who visited Guyana in the 1920s and 30s, showed that after a hundred years the lives of Indians had hardly improved. Andrews was horrified at the conditions of the *logies* on most estates: "Of all the countries I have ever visited, I have never seen anything so bad in this direction, as what I have witnessed in British Guiana." He noted a lax in family life, an "enormous increase" in rum drinking and the steady growth in the number of rum shops. Many of these shops were located near to estate pay offices and were thus easily accessible. He claimed that Indians were losing their self-respect owing to the neglect of their language and culture: "They are not those sturdy villagers whom I know so well in the United Provinces of India and in the Punjab."

The Indian community in Guyana was plagued by other social problems. The most persistent was the refusal of the authorities to recognize Indian marriages performed under Hindu or Muslim rites. The Guyanese authorities, too, were reluctant to enforce the Compulsory Education Act of 1876 in the rural areas, with the result that in the 1930s roughly 62% of Indians were illiterate. In contrast, the illiteracy rate colony-wide was a mere 30%. The request by the Sanatan Dharma Maha Sabha for permission to cremate Indians by the pyre system was also refused for a long time. It was only in 1956 that permission was granted and Dr. Jung

DR. Jung Bahadur Singh
Courtesy of Rajkumari Cultural Center

Bahadur Singh, a former surgeon on emigrants' ships, became the first Indian to be cremated at Plantation Ogle foreshore. In fact, it was Dr. Singh who earlier introduced the bill in the local legislature to permit cremations.

Economic

While a few Indians (landowners, merchants, shopkeepers, lawyers, doctors) became wealthy, the majority of sugar workers lived in dire poverty. For over a hundred years, the minimum pay of 25 cents a day had hardly changed. Besides, sugar workers were overworked, underpaid and often harassed by drivers and their henchmen. Malcolm Buchanan Laing, who became the first Commissioner of Labour in 1933, emphasized that "the only difference between the indentured labourer of old and the free labourer of today was that the former could have been prosecuted if he failed to turn out to work."

The Government of India, too, observed in 1938 that the economic position of Indian workers had "somewhat deteriorated in the last few years." Even many free Indians living off the estates were destitute. Reports noted a sizable number of Indian beggars in Georgetown, "pitiable objects living a hand to mouth existence." They worked mainly as jobbers "picking up a living from any source." The condition of these Indians prompted Kunwar Maharaj Singh to recommend the establishment of a *Dharmsala* (almshouse) to care for them.

The Enmore strike

On 16 June, 1948 at Enmore, the police shot and killed 5 Indian sugar workers and wounded 14 others. The deceased -- Rambarran (aged 30), Lalla Baggee (35), Pooran (30) Surujballi (32) and Harry (30) -- died from shock and hemorrhage caused by bullet wounds. Through the years these workers have been remembered as the 'Enmore Martyrs', a symbol of working class resistance against oppression.

The problem at Enmore started on 22 April between canecutters and the estate management over the newly introduced system of 'cut and load'. This new system required workers to cut the canes and load them into *punts* as one operation. Prior to that, the 'cut and drop' system existed on all sugar estates in the colony. Under the latter, "cane was cut, headed out to the edge of the field and dropped on the parapet of the canal by one gang and then loaded into the *punts* by another." While *punt* loaders received payment by the ton, canecutters were paid by the number of rows of cane cut as estimated by the overseer.

Sugar workers at Enmore strongly opposed the 'cut and load' system. They claimed that the work was dangerous and strenuous and that it resulted in premature aging. They argued that the physically taxing nature of the job was responsible for the reduced number of canecutters on estates. The workers aired other grievances -- shortage of *punts*, nonpayment for canes lost during the weighing process, inaccuracy of the scale, long delays in weighing canes. At the same time (and this infuriated the workers most), wages remained almost the same; 59 cents a ton under 'cut and drop' and 60 cents for cutting and loading as one operation.

While wages remained static, social and economic conditions on estates were getting worse. Good drinking water was in short supply and workers were housed in overcrowded *logies*. The Venn Commission of 1949 condemned housing conditions at Enmore (as Andrews did two decades earlier):

In quite a number the corrugated iron roofs were leaking and the fabric of the buildings were in a general state of decay. In numerous instances temporary sheets or awnings had been fixed over the beds to keep off the rain. They had mud floors and consequently with the rain dropping from the roofs these were made slippery and dangerous.

As the dispute over 'cut and load' heated up, strikes by canecutters and other groups of field workers paralyzed all 7 sugar estates on the East Coast Demerara. On 15 June gangs armed with sticks and cutlasses attacked 2 overseers and 9 nonstrikers who were still working in the fields. The next morning, following a night of unrest in which telegraph posts were uprooted and wooden bridges destroyed, a large crowd gathered at the Enmore factory in an "uncontrollable mood." After the police dispersed them, the workers went to neighboring Non Pareil where they assaulted nonstrikers and overseers. They shouted: "... it is better to sit down and starve, than work and starve."

At about 10 a.m. the action again shifted to Enmore where an estimated 600 workers, led by a man carrying a red flag, approached the factory. With fixed bayonets, the police charged into the crowd. Some of the strikers rushed into the factory, knocked down a Police Constable, seized his rifle and attempted to shoot him. Without reading the Riot Act, the police fired 10 rounds resulting in the death of 5 workers and the wounding of several others.

The shooting was widely condemned. The British Guiana Trades Union Council called for quick justice. The League of Coloured Peoples (which represented the interests of the Black population) blamed the government for its neglect of sugar workers and for "bullying into subjection the native population." The BGEIA criticized the police for failure to read the Riot Act. It felt that early, positive action should have been taken to end the dispute. Speeches by local residents at the Kitty Market Square, a regular meeting place, were most critical of the shooting.

The funeral procession led by Jagan and other Indian leaders was then the largest in Guyana's history. Hundreds assembled at the Enmore estate mortuary to join the procession which, on reaching Plantation Lusignan, had swelled to thousands. The East Coast road was jammed with men, women and children on foot or on bicycles, carts and motor cars. Amid much weeping, threats and resentment, the procession moved peacefully to the Le Repentir Cemetery in Georgetown, a distance of 16 miles.

A few days after the shooting, a Commission of Inquiry headed by Justice F.M. Boland was appointed. The Commission held 26 public sittings at the Victoria Law Courts, visited Enmore and received statements from 92 individuals. Its report concluded that the police were justified in firing at the crowd but that the firing

The Enmore Funeral Procession

"continued in excess of the requirements of the occasion." It admitted, too, that canecutters had a "genuine" grievance over the 'cut and load' system. Furthermore, it questioned the refusal of the sugar planting interests in not seeking the help of the rival union, the Guyana Agricultural (earlier Industrial) Workers Union (GAWU), in settling the dispute.

During the strike the GAWU came into prominence as it vigorously championed the rights of sugar workers. Soon it had overwhelming support in the industry, but the Sugar Producers Association consistently refused to grant recognition. It was only in 1976, when the industry was nationalized, that the GAWU was recognized so as to ensure industrial peace. Of 21,955 votes cast at the polls in the December 1976 elections, the GAWU received 21,487 or 97.9%, the MPCA 376 or 1.71%. An agreement was signed between the union and the sugar bosses, ending 28 years of struggle for recognition in the industry.

The Enmore incident was a landmark in the history of Guyana. A new union emerged which was truly representative of sugar workers. The strike also pushed Jagan into national politics. More importantly, the Enmore incident produced a unity between the two major ethnic groups which blossomed with the victory of the People's Progressive Party (PPP) at the polls in 1953.

Emergence of Cheddi Jagan

It was during the Enmore sugar workers' strike that Jagan, an Indian leader of vision and stature, emerged. Jagan was born on 22 March, 1918 at Plantation Port Mourant on the Corentyne. His parents came from the north Indian state of Uttar Pradesh to work as indentured laborers on the Guyanese sugar plantations. In 1943, after qualifying as a Dentist in the United States, Jagan returned to Guyana. Within two years he became Treasurer of the MPCA. His objection to the high level of allowances, and to the tendency of union leaders to collaborate with the planters, resulted in his removal from his executive post.

The Late Cheddi Jagan, Man of the People

In 1947 Jagan became an elected member of the Legislative Council (chief law making body) for Central Demerara. He thus came in direct contact with sugar workers on the East Coast Demerara. The Enmore shooting certainly affected him as he noted in *The West on Trial*:

At the graveside the emotional outbursts of the widows and relatives of the deceased were intensely distressing, and I could not restrain my tears. There was to be no turning back. There and then I made a silent pledge -- I would dedicate my entire life to the cause of the struggle of the Guianese people against bondage and exploitation.

Jagan's activities during the Enmore strike were resented by government authorities who considered him a "political danger." Consequently, his movements and those of other prominent leaders (Dr. J.P. Latchmansingh, H.J.M. Hubbard, Janet Jagan) were monitored. They were served trespass notices to prevent their entry into strike-bound estates. Such restrictions did not stop them from addressing issues directly affecting sugar workers.

At a public meeting at Grove on the East Bank Demerara, Jagan criticized Governor Charles Woolley: "This Colony has two kings -- King George and King Sugar, the governor supports the latter." At Vryheid's Lust, East Coast Demerara, he outlined the demands of sugar workers -- good medical treatment, proper sanitation and water supply, a balanced diet "not rice and dhall and a little salt fish." He urged strikers to stand firm: "Remember Mahatma Gandhi gave everything he had to see India get her independence. It did not take him a day or two but years."

Jagan, late President of Guyana (1918-1997), was among the first politicians in the Caribbean to draw world attention to the evils of colonialism. An honest, able, gifted and charismatic leader, Jagan raised the national and political consciousness of Guyanese as he fought almost single-handedly in the local legislature against foreign rule. With the formation of the PPP in 1950, Jagan, as leader, provided Guyanese with the first real opportunity to forge national unity.

Jagan's activities as a politician tend to conceal the fact that he was also an accomplished author. His several books, including his classic *The West on Trial*, and dozens of booklets, articles, pamphlets and speeches provide an invaluable record of the social, economic and political history of Guyana. They also reflect Jagan's sound knowledge of national and international affairs.

Political developments

When Guyana came under British control in 1814, the old Dutch constitution remained unchanged. It was not until 1891 that minor constitutional changes were made due largely to pressure from Black leaders. The income qualification for voting remained the same and only males 21 years and over had the right to vote. In 1928 Crown Colony government was introduced mainly to check the power of Black leaders and to preserve the influence and dominance of the Whites. Under this system real power was firmly in the hands of the governor.

It was not until 1953 that a major revision of the constitution occurred. For the first time universal adult suffrage (right to vote given to adults 21 years and over) was introduced. A bicameral (two-house) legislature, consisting of a House of Assembly of 24 elected members and a State Council of 9 nominated members, was set up. Property or income qualifications for elected members were removed but they had to be literate in English. These changes set the stage for a greater involvement of the people in politics and the emergence of mass political parties in Guyana.

By the late 1940s over 20 trade unions representing various categories of workers were registered. Although trade union leaders were involved in politics, they made little attempt to organize political parties. It was in 1946 that Jagan, his wife Janet, Hubbard and Ashton Chase formed the Political Affairs Committee. In 1950 the PPP was formed out of the old Political Affairs Committee. Jagan became leader and L.F.S. Burnham, a young, Black barrister who returned to the colony in 1949, became chairman. They were able, at least for a short time, to unite both Indians and Blacks into a political force.

By the early 1950s the PPP grew in popularity and strength. In the general elections of April 1953 it won 51% of the votes and gained 18 out of the 24 seats in the House of Assembly. Expectations ran high as the PPP was seen as the party which would bring about national unity and prosperity. By the end of the year, however, the constitution was suspended and some of the leaders imprisoned. The British Government listed several reasons for its unexpected action. It accused the PPP leaders of instigating strikes, attempting to silence trade union leaders, flooding the colony with communist literature, spreading racial hatred, neglect of duties and of undermining the loyalty of the police.

The suspension of the constitution seemed to stem from conflicts which soon developed between PPP leaders and the colonial governor. Two bills proposed by the PPP brought matters to a head. One, the Rice Farmers' Security of Tenure Bill, sought to protect farmers against steep rent increases and to require landlords to provide adequate drainage and carry out necessary improvements. What seemed to alarm the governor and the sugar interests, the largest landowners in the colony, was the provision which gave the district commissioner the power to sell the properties of those who refused to pay for improvements. The bill was passed in the House of Assembly. It was, however, rejected in the State Council where the nominated members were in a majority. This situation tended to worsen the conflict.

The other bill, the Labour Relations Bill, was geared to settle the dispute in the sugar industry between the MPCA and GAWU regarding recognition. Continuing inter-union rivalry and strikes demanded action to bring about peace and stability in the industry. The bill provided for mandatory recognition, by secret ballot, of trade unions which enjoyed overwhelming support in the industry. The bill was bitterly opposed by the MPCA which, though recognized by the sugar interests, had little support among sugar workers. On 8 October, 1953 the bill was passed in the House of Assembly. The next day British troops landed and the PPP was thrown out of the government after only 133 days in office. The PPP government was accused of turning the colony into a communist satellite and attempting to control the trade union movement. An Interim Government was then set up to govern the colony.

In the beginning of 1955 Burnham's attempt to take control of the PPP led to a split in the party -- one faction headed by Burnham and the other by Jagan. In the 1957 general elections, which both factions contested, Jagan's faction won 9 of the 14 seats and Burnham's 3. The minor parties -- the United Democratic Party led by John Carter, and the National Labour Front headed by Lionel Luckhoo -- won one seat each. Jagan was invited to form the government and to name five ministers to serve in the Governor's Executive Council.

Soon afterwards Burnham renamed his faction the People's National Congress (PNC) and began to court the support of Black and Portuguese leaders. The brief unity of the two major ethnic groups came to an end as the PNC was seen as a party for Blacks and the PPP for Indians.

The elections of 1961 witnessed violent and ugly racial conflicts. The PPP won 20 of the 35 seats, the PNC 11 and the United Force (UF) led by Portuguese businessman, Peter D'Aguiar, 4. Jagan, now designated Premier, formed the new government. Between 1962 and 1964 several anti-PPP elements worked to undermine the government and to ensure its downfall.

As the Cold War (1945-1991) between the two superpowers waged on, the Kennedy administration became alarmed at Jagan's socialist policies and close ties with Fidel Castro of Cuba. The United States Government reportedly used the Central Intelligence Agency (CIA) to instigate strikes and riots. Strong opposition was shown to the government's budget which was prepared by Nicholas Kaldor, an English economist and tax expert. This Kaldor budget was geared to reform the tax system so that the wealthy would pay more. Both Burnham and D'Aguiar gathered their supporters for a showdown with the government. When the government introduced the Labour Relations Bill in March 1963, similar to the one proposed in 1953, the Trades Union Council called a strike which lasted 80 days.

The strike witnessed the worst racial violence in Guyana's history. The victims were both Indians and perceived supporters of the government. Indians going about their business peacefully were accosted, robbed and beaten. Indian homes were ransacked and set on fire and several business places were looted and burnt. In fact, anyone suspected of being a government supporter was attacked. In Georgetown and elsewhere, civil servants and others who refused to go on strike were beaten and robbed and their homes looted. The burning of homes and raping of women forced many Indians to flee to other parts of the country where they set up squatter schemes. Even government ministers were not spared. The strike ended when the government agreed not to reintroduce the Labour Relations Bill in its original form. To the dismay of anti-government elements, the strike did not bring down the PPP government.

It was the role played by the United States, and Britain to a lesser extent, which directly brought the downfall of Jagan. The CIA was alleged to have spent over a million dollars to finance the strike which helped the strikers to make new demands on the government. The American Government also pressured the British Government to change the electoral system from 'first-past-the-post' to Proportional Representation. This change served only to intensify the racial problem. The United States Government was convinced that a change in the electoral system would remove the PPP from office. It did just that.

In the elections of 7 December, 1964 the PPP received 45.8% of the votes and 24 out of 53 seats, the PNC 40.5% and 22 seats and the U.F. 12.4% and 7 seats. A PNC-UF coalition formed the government. The PNC subsequently induced several members of the PPP and UF to join it and thus gained control over the government. For the next 28 years the PNC retained power through a combination of fear, intimidation and rigged national elections. This period witnessed the 'second migration' of Indians to North America and elsewhere.

The 'second' migration

By October 1992 when the PNC was voted out of office in the first free and fair election since independence, it was estimated that Guyana had lost more than one-third of its population. Guyanese were protesting against the PNC regime by 'voting with their feet'. The majority of Guyanese migrated to the United States, Canada, Suriname and the Caribbean Islands. Three main factors influenced such migration overseas -- economic, political, educational concerns.

Economic

Quality of life under the PNC got progressively worse. The daily minimum wage ($15.10 in 1984) was barely enough to buy a pint of cooking oil. The cost of living skyrocketed and inflation was way out of control. By the end of 1986 the unemployment rate was more than 30%.

The shortage of basic food (dal, rice, sugar, wheat flour, cooking oil) became a way of life. Guyanese would stand in long lines for hours at the government-controlled food distribution centers in a desperate bid to survive. Waiting in lines for basic food resulted in absenteeism and low productivity. It was estimated in 1981 that the infantile mortality rate was an alarming 42.7 per 1000.

The rice industry, dominated by Indians, suffered most during this period. The withdrawal of duty free concession and easy credit to rice farmers led many to stop growing rice. At the same time increasing export of rice, largely to obtain foreign exchange, led to a shortage in the local market. Rice which was available for the local market was of inferior quality and hardly fit for human consumption.

In addition to food shortages, the lack of basic facilities produced frustration and anger. Electrical blackouts, termed 'load shedding', occurred on a daily basis, resulting in damage to electrical appliances. During these periods of blackout government offices were either shut or did little business transactions.

Blackouts provided cover for organized gangs of thugs to kick down doors of private homes and rob and rape innocent Guyanese.

Despite its many rivers, Guyana also suffered from an acute shortage of good drinking water. In Georgetown, low pressure and burst mains meant considerable difficulty in obtaining water for cooking and other domestic chores. Residents in the rural areas regularly traveled miles for a bucket of water. Pollutants in the water often led to gastroenteritis and death.

High inflation, low wages, an increasing cost of living, poor social services and a deteriorating quality of life provided an important inducement to leave Guyana for greener pastures. Even those earning comparatively higher wages (university professors, teachers, policemen, civil servants) experienced economic hardships. Since it was difficult to sustain life, many realized that they would be vulnerable at retirement. To thousands of Guyanese of all races, emigration seemed the only alternative.

Political

During this period Indians, in particular, fell victims to widespread racial discrimination. Such discrimination was clearly noticeable in the rice industry. In the 1950s and 60s the development of the rice industry by Indians made it the leading sector of the economy after sugar and bauxite. The industry made important advances and farmers received a guaranteed price for rice and paddy.

After 1964 the PNC government adopted a program which not only discriminated against Indians but also seriously affected agricultural development. One of its first acts was to cut off the favorable trade with Cuba. Soon guaranteed prices for rice were reduced and duty free concession for gasoline, insecticides and spare parts was withdrawn. The Rice Marketing Board fell into the hands of government supporters who allegedly cheated the farmers in the weighing and grading of their rice. The neglect of drainage and irrigation placed farmers' produce at the mercy of floods. It was also frequently alleged that rice plots were taken away from Indian farmers and given to PNC supporters.

These discriminatory practices led to low morale among many farmers who were forced to migrate overseas. Consequently, rice production decreased year after year. From being the 'breadbasket' of the Caribbean, Guyana became the 'basket case' of the Caribbean. The situation even affected many Guyanese abroad who were ashamed to identify themselves as Guyanese. Guyana soon became the butt of an industry of jokes.

Racism was also observed in the sugar industry after nationalization. The government condemned the practice of using the profits of the sugar industry to subsidize housing schemes for sugar workers. Such a practice was understandable since sugar workers generated the profits with their blood, sweat and tears. Instead, the profits of sugar were switched to areas unconnected with the industry, particularly where PNC supporters lived. Additionally, the majority of administrative positions in the industry were given to government supporters who had little or limited experience of the process of sugar manufacture.

Soon after coming to power the PNC government practically unleashed 'a reign of terror' on the opposition, particularly the PPP and the Working People Alliance led by the eminent Black historian, Dr. Walter Rodney. Both Indians and Blacks suffered violent beatings by organized gangs of thugs. They targeted largely Indian homes; kicking down doors, raping women and girls, robbing and killing other members of the family. It was claimed that gang members wore military boots and carried semi-automatic weapons, implying that they were probably members of the country's armed forces. Members of the House of Israel, led by a fugitive from the United States, were allegedly armed and supported by the government. The leader of the House of Israel, Rabbi Washington, openly admitted that he was instructed by senior PNC ministers to attack the opposition. They regularly broke up legitimate strikes and disrupted meetings held by the opposition.

Besides, the government repeatedly rigged successive elections to stay in power. A team of international observers reported several irregularities in the 1980 elections. They found that the entire polling process was in the hands of PNC supporters and that eligible voters were denied the right to vote. They reported grave abuse of proxy and postal voting. Besides, there were several instances of 'busing' government supporters from one polling booth to another which meant multiple voting. The observers concluded that the 1980 election was "rigged massively and flagrantly." Cases of the armed forces highjacking and tampering with ballot boxes were frequently reported.

During the 28 years of PNC dictatorship, Indians generally felt "left out." Many saw their salvation in emigration. An informed eye-witness summed up the situation: "Racial discrimination and 'second class' status have been the lot of Indians [who] ... suffer doubly: from discrimination because of their race and culture; from exploitation as members of the working class and peasantry."

Educational concerns

In 1976 the Burnham government committed itself to providing free education from kindergarten to university. Free education thus became available to many who previously could not afford the high cost. However, as time went on the standard of education showed a steady decline. Most of the school buildings were in a poor state of repair. There was a constant shortage of books, furniture and science equipment. Morale in the teaching profession fell so low that a sizable number of professionally qualified teachers quit their jobs to teach in the Caribbean Islands, particularly Jamaica, the U.S. Virgin Islands and the Bahamas.

Racial discrimination in the teaching profession also forced many teachers, including headmasters on the verge of retirement, to emigrate. Those teachers, particularly Indians, who expressed concern at prevailing conditions were either dismissed or transferred. The decline in the quality of education led to an increase in the rate of illiteracy as unqualified, untrained teachers replaced those who migrated abroad. Results at the London General Certificate of Education Examination (GCE) were so consistently poor that embarrassed officials refused to publish them. (This examination was taken at the end of a five-year course at the secondary level.)

Even the University of Guyana suffered from a loss of qualified staff on account of direct political interference. Professors who criticized the regime were either denied appointment or dismissed through nonrenewal of contracts. The most glaring example of political interference in education was the case of Rodney. This renowned Professor of African History was denied appointment as Head of the History Department although the Appointments Committee offered him the job.

The introduction of National Service as a requirement for graduation at the University of Guyana seemed to affect Indians more than the other groups. Many young people and their parents were skeptical about the motives of National Service, having learned of reports of sexual misconduct. As a result, many Indian women preferred to go overseas to pursue higher education.

This 'second migration' had a negative impact on Guyana's development. The shortage of skilled personnel meant that a large number of expatriates had to be hired at salaries and fringe benefits which the country could hardly afford. The shortage of trained, qualified teachers was reflected in poor performance in mathematics, science and other subjects at the regional CXC Examination which replaced the GCE. The migration of farmers led to a shortage of rice and other agricultural products as well as higher prices which fueled inflation. In general, the lack of skilled personnel had hindered many development projects. Efforts to encourage qualified Guyanese to return home have so far met with mixed results.

To sum up, worsening economic conditions, racial discrimination, falling education standards and lack of fair and free elections contributed to the movement of Guyanese overseas. Some Guyanese, desperate to leave, spent thousands of dollars to enter the United States and Canada illegally through the 'back track.' Although conditions have improved since 1992, the movement overseas continues.

Indian contributions

The sugar industry

In the 1840s the planters' greatest fear was that the sugar industry would collapse from want of labor. Some 50 years later, this cry of "ruin" was replaced by one of prosperity as sugar output trebled. The labor of indentured Indians was certainly a factor in this prosperity. Indians provided that cheap, reliable labor without which the sugar industry could hardly have survived the competition from slave-owning colonies like Cuba and Brazil. Wages remained very low and conditions were akin to slavery.

As early as 1848 Governor Henry Barkly, an estate proprietor, admitted that without Indian labor the sugar industry would have collapsed. William Russell, attorney and proprietor, saw Indian immigration as "a matter of life and death importance to the Colony." Crosby later underlined the Indian contribution to the prosperity of sugar with more force: "To the thews and sinews of the East Indian Coolie, Demerara owes its present leading position as a sugar-producing colony." Indians, too, were conscious of their contribution. When told by a Black worker to "clear out" of Guyana, an Indian reminded him that Black workers were at one time starving and that it was Indian labor which saved the sugar industry from collapse. This Indian worker knew what he was talking about as he had probably arrived in Guyana with the first batch.

Agriculture

The most vital and sustained Indian contribution is the development of agriculture. From the 1870s Indians began to leave the plantations and establish themselves on small holdings with agriculture as the main occupation. Very quickly Indians, the majority belonging to the agricultural castes, began to dominate cattle and dairy farming, coconut farming and the rice industry.

Cattle and dairy farming

As Indians slowly moved out of the plantations, cattle rearing became a primary occupation. At first it was carried on mostly on the estates as this was an important inducement to keep time-expired Indians in the colony. The two main areas of cattle farming were the Corentyne savannahs and west Berbice. By the first two decades of the 20th century, Indians owned more head of cattle than any other group.

The profitable milk trade was completely dominated by Indians. They sold the milk to fellow Indians who did not own cattle, to estate hospitals and to Black villagers and urban dwellers. Cattle owners also consumed large quantities of milk. They often turned the milk into *dahi* (curds/yogurt) which was a part of their diet. The Indian attachment to his cow was depicted in a cartoon in the local press. The manager of an estate met Jugdeo who was sobbing loudly: "What's matter, Jugdeo, you so much cry? You wife dead?" asked the manager. "No, manja," replied Jugdeo, "me no choopid man go cry um suppose wife dead. Me cow dead."

Coconut farming

Although climatic conditions have been suitable for coconut cultivation, the industry only reached some importance when Indians became involved at the beginning of the 20th century. With Indian participation, exports of coconut oil steadily increased. One important reason in the growth of the industry was that Indians consumed more coconut oil than the rest of the population. Today Indians use coconut oil in cooking, in religious observances, on their hair and on their body to give it a shiny appearance. They use the kernel for making cakes and puddings and the husk as a source of fuel. They also turn the branches of the coconut tree into brooms for sweeping their homes and surroundings.

Rice farming

The most important Indian contribution was their development of the rice industry. Consequently, Guyana quickly became the leading rice producer in the Caribbean. The main rice producing regions were, and still are, the Essequibo including the islands of Leguan and Wakenaam, Mahaica-Abary in Central Demerara and the upper Corentyne coast. From the start, rice was grown on estate lands; later, on lands leased or purchased by Indians. From the early 20th century rice cultivation progressively increased. By the end of indenture, over 1,400 tons of rice were exported. Between 1993 and 1996 exports of rice jumped from 124,000 to 300,000 tons.

There were several reasons for the steady growth of the rice industry. The most important was the availability of cheap land which was turned into rice cultivation. The recurrent famines in India, which was Guyana's main rice supplier, and the outbreak of World War I were other crucial factors. As a result of the war and the consequent high price of imported flour, rice became the chief means of subsistence. Besides being consumed by Indians and Chinese, rice soon became the staple food of other sections of the Guyanese population.

The progress of the rice industry, however, contrasted with the "semi-slavery" conditions of the growers. Many suffered from over-exhaustion and were subject to frequent attacks of malaria. It was claimed that mortality in the Indian community was highest among rice growers. The millers, on the other hand, became wealthy as they exploited the growers largely through high interest rates and high land rentals.

It was from this Indian middle class (landlords, millers, money lenders, milk distributors, urban merchants and professionals) that Indian leadership began to emerge. They realized the importance of an English education even if it meant conversion to Christianity. As their children acquired a proficiency in English, they joined the civil service or pursued training abroad particularly in law and medicine. In the 1920s some of the successful members of the Indian middle class included Ramsaroop Maraj, Rash Beharry, Resaul Maraj, Caramat Ali Macdoom, Seetahal, Hanooman Singh, Thomas Flood, Francis Kawall and K.P. Das.

Other contributions

Besides these various contributions, Indians set an example of thrift and industry which enabled them to survive and to acquire small fortunes as well. Indian enterprise, their commitment to the family and a will to achieve ensured their progress in agriculture. Indians also introduced a rich and different culture into the Caribbean. The Indian ritual marriage form and the extended family system continued with few major changes. Indians brought a variety of music, art forms and amusement which quickly took root. Indian foods like roti and curry, dal, *keer* (rice pudding) and *takari* (vegetable dishes) are regularly consumed by almost every ethnic group in the Guyanese society.

Indians also opened up new occupations. One traditional occupation was money lending which *banias* (the money lending and business castes of India) dominated. The scarcity of banks and their distant location in the towns made money lending vital in the Indian community. Through high rates of interest, *banias* became very wealthy. Some Indians, too, made small fortunes through investment in gold and jewelry. Many melted down silver coins into jewelry with which they bedecked their wives and children. The growth of Indian village settlements in the coastal belt gave rise to Indian participation in several other crafts.

Many of the Indian contributions like the traditional art form and the dance dramas disappeared with time. But Indian contributions to thought in economic and political matters survived. In the economic field, their dedication to agriculture helped to support a vital sector of the economy and made Guyana the food bowl of the Caribbean. In the political field, they introduced the *Panchayat* system whereby a local council of five elders dealt with all matters in the Indian village. This system of community government tended to bond Indians and to defend the system of local government against the central government.

Indians in New York City

Indians from the Caribbean have been migrating to the United States and Canada in considerable numbers since the 1960s. The early batches left largely to improve their educational or professional qualifications. The later batches, called 'new immigrants', have different educational backgrounds and aspirations. A conservative estimate shows that between 150,000 and 200,000 documented and undocumented Caribbean Indians are living in NYC.

Like all minority immigrant groups (Chinese, Italians, Greeks, Russians, Cubans, Indians from the sub-continent), Caribbean Indians in NYC tend to concentrate in certain areas. In the Bronx, they concentrate between 161st Street and Kingsbridge; in Brooklyn, at Greenpoint and Cypress Hills; in Queens, at Richmond Hill, Jamaica, Ozone Park and Queens Village. Those who have resettled in Florida also concentrate in certain areas in Orlando, Miami and Fort Lauderdale. Smaller numbers also live in Minnesota, New Jersey, Texas and Maryland. These settlement patterns are influenced largely by friends and families already resident there. They tend to provide temporary shelter and financial help to enable the 'new immigrants' to start anew. In such an alien environment, a sense of security and community is important to the new arrivals.

Adjustment to life in a new society is often very difficult. While many Caribbean Indians in NYC have adapted quickly, others have found city life a traumatic experience, particularly as Caribbean Indians are largely rural dwellers. One of the greatest problems which these 'new immigrants' face is the difficulty of finding a job which matches their educational and professional qualifications. As a result, many become self-employed in a variety of fields (real estate, insurance, retail, construction and auto body repairs). A small number of medical doctors, dentists, lawyers and accountants have set up private practice in Richmond Hill.

The majority of Indians are employed in the private and public sectors. Very few have pursued the teaching profession in the NYC public school system. The long and frustrating certification process, inadequate pay, perceived discrimination in the hiring process and poor discipline among students have contributed to a lack of interest in teaching. Experienced, qualified Caribbean

Indo-Guyanese Performers in
'PUSHPANJALI', A Rajkumari Center Production, 1996

Photography: Nala Singham

Indian teachers tend to turn either to real estate or insurance sales for a livelihood.

As in many immigrant societies, some Caribbean Indians have been unable to adjust to the new life. Because of advanced qualifications, they tend to shun jobs which they consider demeaning. Depression often drives them either back to the Caribbean or to other states. On the other hand, those with suitable jobs are highly valued by their employers because of their reliability and productivity. Like other immigrant groups, they send money home to enable families to meet daily living expenses, to renovate their homes, purchase a car or buy a piece of land for farming.

One of the features of Hinduism and Islam is the ability to adapt to the new environment. In NYC the growth of Mandirs and Mosques provides clear evidence of the survival of these two religions. Initially, religious services are held in the basement of private homes. Later, permanent structures are built largely through fund-raising activities and private donations by devotees. Some of the religious organizations include the America Sevashram Sangha, the Arya Spiritual Center, the Shiva Mandir, the Maha Lakshmi Mandir and the Shri Lakshmi Narayan Mandir. The prominent Mosques include Masjid Al-Abidin and Masjid Omar Ben Abdel-Aziz.

By establishing religious and cultural organizations, Caribbean Indians have been able not only to keep tradition alive but also to recreate their Caribbean lifestyle. Their traditional food (rice, curry, roti, spices, dal, chillies) are readily available and regularly consumed. Curry and roti shops have mushroomed on Liberty Avenue and in other areas where Indians concentrate. The songs of Rafi, Lata, Kishore, Mukesh and others, as well as those of several local artistes, are regularly heard. Prominent Indian TV and radio personalities host a variety of programs on Indian culture and religion. However, some of these TV personalities, in their zeal to enhance their career and promote the business of their sponsors, produce programs which depict Indian culture in a negative and demeaning way. Indian festivals are observed often with more

The Phagwah March in Richmond Hill, Queens

The Diwali March in Richmond Hill, Queens

fervor than in the Caribbean. The annual Phagwah march on Liberty Avenue attracts upwards of 5,000 Caribbean Indians and others.

But the picture is not altogether rosy. The children of Caribbean Indians face serious adjustment problems. Coming from a society where standard English is not commonly spoken, many of these students are reluctant to participate in class discussions. Not only are they mockingly referred to as 'Gandhi,' or 'Mohamed,' but also they are often ridiculed for their accents. Those who are sensitive to jeers sometimes cut classes or drop out of school. Others bow to peer pressure, change their names, dye their hair or avoid contact with other Indo-Caribbean students.

In the school system Indian students also suffer from poor placement by school administrators who have inadequate knowledge of the British education system. As such, little effort is made to evaluate accurately the academic attainment of these students. Consequently, those who are not fluent in spoken English are incorrectly labeled 'learning disabled' and placed in Special Education classes. Many of these students soon become frustrated as they find their placement demeaning. Even those who have already completed their secondary education and passed the stringent CXC examination are similarly misplaced. The motivation to remain in school soon disappears as these students regularly complain that the education standard is lower than that in the Caribbean.

While Caribbean Indians generally have improved their economic status, the community is hopelessly divided and factionalism is widespread. The community suffers from a lack of honest, sincere, dedicated leaders. The self-appointed leaders, who are poor role models, are jostling for power, position and prestige, ignoring issues which are bound to affect future generations. Despite successes in business and in the professions, the Indo-Caribbean community has no representation in either local, city, state or national government. Without political representation, the community has no clout. Even 'spiritual' leaders have become 'little Caesars' , and there seems to be deep divisions in the Hindu community -- between Sanatanists and Samajists.

To sum up, there is improvement generally in the economic position of Caribbean Indians. The social problems, however, continue to mount. Many parents are 'losing' their children who become victims to inner city vices (alcoholism, substance abuse, truancy, gang warfare). Very often children are left without parental supervision resulting in a high rate of school drop out and absenteeism. A more disturbing trend is the increasing number of divorces and teenage pregnancies. On the other hand, there are a number of success stories among Indo-Caribbean students in a variety of fields. As the community grows larger, the need for political representation to enable it to gain influence and power becomes more pressing than ever.

Conclusion

From the time of their arrival in Guyana, Indian workers were degraded and exploited. As indentured workers, every aspect of their lives was controlled. The planters fixed the wages and hours of labor and even restricted the movements of workers. When Indians protested against harsh working and living conditions, they were subject to arrest, fines, imprisonment and expulsion from the estate. That they were able to survive was due to their resilience, custom, tradition and commitment to the family which promoted thrift, industry and a cooperative spirit. Their culture tended to boost their self-esteem and foster a strong desire to achieve. Indian culture became the most lasting and continuous form of resistance against the plantation system.

Even when indenture was abolished, the planters continued to exploit sugar workers. Consequently, the economic position of Indians a century after their arrival had improved little. The Victorian virtues of thrift and industry enabled some to establish their independence from the estate and to build up their own resources. The novelist, George Lamming, stressed this aspect of their contribution: "They are, perhaps, our only jewels of a true and native thrift and industry. They have taught us by example the value of money; for they respect money as only people with a high sense of communal responsibility can."

Power Aims

1. Should the history of Caribbean Indians be taught in NYC High Schools?
2. Could slavery in the Caribbean be justified?
3. Did slave emancipation change the relationship between workers and employers?
4. Was the attempt by the sugar planters to keep workers on their plantations successful?
5. Did immigration answer the problem of labor supply for the planters?
6. Did recruiters abuse the recruiting system?
7. Did conditions on the voyage encourage high mortality?
8. Should Indians be welcomed by the Black population?
9. Were Indians exploited by the planters?
10. Was the caste system destined to disappear?
11. Was religion a blessing or a curse on Indians?
12. Were wife murders the result of a shortage of women?
13. Were strikes on estates inevitable?
14. Was the movement to abolish indenture similar to the British anti-slavery movement of the early 19th century?
15. Could the Indian policy of neutrality be justified?
16. Was indenture a new form of slavery?
17. Could the Enmore strike have been prevented?
18. Were Indian sugar workers docile?
19. Did Cheddi Jagan have a place in Guyanese/Caribbean History?
20. Should politicians be blamed for Guyana's problems?
21. Should the United States welcome Caribbean Indians as immigrants?
22. Is it easy or difficult for Caribbean Indians to adjust to life in NYC?
23. Is Richmond Hill "Little Guyana"?
24. Should Caribbean Indians assimilate into American society?
25. Are the social problems faced by Caribbean Indians inevitable?

26. Should Caribbean Indians continue to migrate to the United States?
27. Is the education system in NYC High Schools better or worse than in the Caribbean?
28. Have the lifestyles of Caribbean Indians changed for the better or worse?
29. Is the Caribbean Indian community in NYC a divided one?
30. Would the culture of Caribbean Indians survive in NYC?

GLOSSARY

Amerindians   the original inhabitants of Guyana. They are divided into four main tribes.

Andamans   a group of islands in the Bay of Bengal where convicts were housed; a place of no return.

arkati   an unlicensed recruiter in northern India.

Arya Samaj   a religious organization founded in 1875 by Swami Dayanand Saraswati. It advocated social reforms like the education of women and an end to child marriage.

bania   a Hindu trader or money lender.

beeraha   song/dance performed at weddings and melas

Bengalis   those immigrants in northern India who were shipped to the sugar colonies from the port of Calcutta.

bhajans   Hindu religious songs.

Bhojpuris   immigrants recruited from the districts of western Bihar and eastern Uttar Pradesh.

Brahmins   composed of priests and teachers; the highest caste among Hindus. .Hindu society is divided into four castes -- Brahmins, Kshatriyas, Vaishyas and Sudras.

chaprasi   messenger in a government office or other establishment. He also accompanied recruits traveling by train from northern India to the Calcutta depot.

Charak Puja   also known as hook-swinging or the wheel form of worship. It was a fertility ritual.

Chota Nagpur   a subdivision of the Bengal
Presidency about 200-300 miles from Calcutta.

chowtals   religious songs which Hindus sing during Phagwah.

compounders   they dispensed medicines, assisted the ship's surgeon in supervising emigrants on the voyage and often acted as interpreters.

coolies   a derogatory term currently in use to describe Indians.

creoles   the term is used generally to describe those of African descent born in Guyana.

dal   yellow split peas which form a regular part of the Indian diet.

dand-tal   a 40 inch bronze metal stick beaten with another small curved metal one; a musical instrument.

Deepavali   Hindu festival of lights.

dhoti traditional dress of Indian men.

dollar equivalent to four shillings and two pence.

Eid Muslim religious festival.

ghee clarified butter made from milk.

headman leader or driver.

Hill Coolies the various tribes inhabiting the rugged Chota Nagpur plateau.

Holi colorful Hindu religious festival commemorating the triumph of good over evil; the beginning of spring.

jhumar song/dance of the tribal people.

kala pani black water; the name of dread by which Indians designate the sea.

kitchen garden small plot of land given to slaves (and later to Indians) so that they could feed themselves and keep estate expenditure down.

Krishna Janamashtmi celebration of the birth of Lord Krishna.

logies long, wooden ranges formerly occupied by slaves and subsequently by indentured workers.

Madrasis generally immigrants from south India shipped to the sugar colonies from the port of Madras.

Mahabharata an epic poem of ancient India; besides its narrative, it also conveys folklore and philosophy.

maistris unlicensed recruiters in south India.

mandir a Hindu temple.

megass remains of the cane after the juice has been extracted.

mosque a Muslim temple.

moulvi a Muslim priest.

nagara song/dance of the cowherds.

pass ticket of leave; a document, signed by the manager, showing that the indentured worker was legally entitled to leave the plantation temporarily.

pundit a Hindu priest.

punt flat-bottomed iron boat used to convey cane from the field to the factory.

Ramayana Hindu religious text which tells of the life of Lord Rama.

Ram Naumi birth celebration of Lord Rama.

ring leaders strike leaders who protested loudly against working conditions.

Riot Act required reading by the police or magistrate telling strikers to disperse before the use of force.

rupee a sum representing about two shillings (48 cents).

Sanatan Dharma Maha Sabha an organization formed to counter the influence of the Arya Samaj.

sarangi stringed musical instrument.

sari traditional dress of Indian women.

shoveling digging of trenches, a job which required physical strength.

Sita Jayanti birth celebration of Sita.

subagent Indian or European who managed a subagency which recruited laborers in northern India.

tadjah Hosein in Trinidad and Hosay in Jamaica. A mourning ritual commemorating the martyrdom of Husain and Hasan, sons of Ali and grandsons of the Prophet Mohammed. The ritual originated in Iraq but was later observed in India and then brought to the Caribbean by Muslim immigrants.

Tamils indentured workers from south India. During this period thousands of south Indians migrated to neighboring Ceylon (Sri Lanka).

ton equivalent to 2,240 pounds.

topazees sweepers on board emigrant ships. They comprised men of different nationalities recruited in grog shops and with little means of support.

tassa traditional drum.

vacuum pans an innovation installed on estates which produced better quality sugar. By this method the sugar was dried faster.

Further reading

Adamson, A.H. *Sugar Without Slaves. The Political Economy of British Guiana, 1838-1904.* London, 1972.

Beaumont, J. *The New Slavery: An Account of the Indian and Chinese Immigrants in British Guiana.* London, 1871.

Birbalsingh, F. (ed.). *Indo Caribbean Resistance.* Toronto, 1993.

_____. *From Pillar to Post. The Indo-Caribbean Diaspora.* Toronto, 1997.

Bronkhurst, H.V.P. *The Colony of British Guiana and its Labouring Population.* London, 1883.

Dabydeen, D. and Samaroo, B. (eds.)
India in the Caribbean. London, 1987.

Depoo, T. (ed.). *The East Indian Diaspora.* New York, 1993.

Jagan, C.B. *The West on Trial.* London, 1966.

Jenkins, E.J. *The Coolie: His Rights and Wrongs.* London, 1871.

Mangru, B. *Benevolent Neutrality. Indian Government Policy and Labour Migration to British Guiana, 1854-1884.* London, 1987.

_____. *Indenture and Abolition. Sacrifice and Survival on the Guyanese sugar plantations.* Toronto, 1993.

_____. *A History of East Indian Resistance on the Guyana sugar estates, 1869-1948.* New York, 1996.

Naipaul, V. *An Area of Darkness: An experience of India.* London, 1964.

_____. *India: A Wounded Civilization.* London, 1977.

Nath, D. *History of Indians in British Guiana.* 2nd. edn. London, 1970.

Ruhoman, P. *Centenary History of the Indians in British Guiana, 1838-1938.* London, 1947.

Seecharan, C. *'Tiger in the Stars'. An Anatomy of Indian Achievement in British Guiana 1919-1929.* London, 1997.

Singh, C. *Guyana. Politics in a Plantation Society.* New York, 1988.

Tinker, H.A. *A New System of Slavery. The Export of Indian Labour Overseas, 1820-1930.* Oxford, 1974.

Wood, D. *Trinidad in Transition. The Years after Slavery.* Oxford, 1968.

Journals, Periodicals, Seminar Papers

Gillion, K.L. 'The Sources of Indian Emigration to Fiji'. *Population Studies,* 10 (Nov. 1956): 139-157.

Mangru, B. 'Indenture: Paternalism or neo-Slavery?' *Release,* (Sept. 1978): 37-42.

_____ 'James Crosby: Hero, Protector, Friend of Indians in Guyana'. *Indo-Caribbean Review,* 1:1 (1994): 29-65.

_____ 'The sex-ratio disparity and its consequences under the indenture system in British Gu iana'. *India in the Caribbean.* London, 1987, pp. 211-230.

_____ 'Tadjah in British Guiana. Manipulation or Protest'. *Indo-Caribbean Resistance.* Toronto, 1993, pp. 13-26.

_____ 'Aftermath of Indenture. The British Guiana Colonization Scheme, 1915-1927'. *Journal of Caribbean Studies,* 5:3 (1986): 181-198.

_____ 'Hook-Swinging in Mid-Nineteenth Century Guyana'. *History Gazette,* 4&5 (1992-1993): 22-31.

_____ 'Disparity in Bengal and Madras Emigration to British Guiana'. *Revista/Review Interamericana,* XIII, 1-4 (1987): 99-107.

_____ 'Abolishing the return passage entitlement under indenture. Guianese planter pressure and Indian Government response'. *Caribbean Quarterly,* 32, 3&4 (Sept.-Dec. 1986): 1-13.

_____ 'Indian Government policy towards labor recruitment for the sugar colonies, 1838-1883'. *Journal of Third World Studies,* IX, 1 (Spring, 1992): 118-138.

Moore, B.L. 'The Retention of Caste Notions among the Indian Immigrants in British Guiana during the Nineteenth Century'. *Comparative Studies in Society and History,* 19:1 (Jan. 1977): 96-107.

Powell, J.H. 'Hook-Swinging in India'. *Folklore,* 25 (1914): 147-197.

Roberts, G.W. and Bryne, J. 'Summary Statistics on Indenture and Associated Migration affecting the West Indies 1834-1918'. *Population Studies,* 20:1 (July, 1966): 125-134.

Index

107